体验汉语®短期教程
Experiencing Chinese Short-Term Course

商务篇 (60—80课时)
Business Communication in China

修订版

英语版

主编 张红 岳薇

高等教育出版社·北京

《体验汉语®》立体化系列教材

短期教程（修订版）

总 策 划　刘　援

顾　　问　刘　珣

策 划 编 辑　梁　宇

项 目 编 辑　杨　曦

编写委员会（按姓名音序排列）

　　　　　陈作宏　　褚佩如　　高　莹　　吕宇红

　　　　　孙　易　　田　艳　　汪梦川　　岳建玲

　　　　　岳　薇　　张　红　　张如梅　　朱晓星

本 册 主 编　张　红　　岳　薇

本 册 审 译　Jeremy Rubinstein　　Lyric Grimes

前言

"体验汉语短期教程"自 2005 年陆续出版以来,受到全球数以万计的汉语教师和学习者的关注和喜爱。为顺应时代变化,紧跟汉语教学的快速发展,编写组在对该系列的使用情况进行广泛调研、认真听取一线教师的宝贵建议后,对该系列教程进行了全面修订和完善。

该系列教程的编写理念是什么?

遵循"体验式语言学习"的理念,强调"做中学、体验中学",用活动贯穿课堂,提供丰富有趣的练习、活动、游戏、歌曲等,营造愉悦的汉语学习氛围,持续激发学生的学习兴趣。

该系列教程的适用对象有哪些?

适用于中国高校和汉语教学机构短期来华留学生、外交人员及其他外籍人士,也适用于孔子学院、孔子课堂、华文学校等海外汉语教学机构短期汉语学习者。

该系列教程由哪些分册构成?

该系列共七册,涵盖海内外短期汉语课程的主要专题。各篇难度及课时安排列表如下:

篇名	难度	课时安排
《留学篇》	零起点	50—70 课时
《生活篇》	零起点	40—50 课时
《生活篇·进阶》	已完成大约 50 课时的基础汉语学习	60—80 课时
《旅游篇》	已完成大约 50 课时的基础汉语学习	40—50 课时
《文化篇》	已完成大约 160 课时的基础汉语学习	60—80 课时
《商务篇》	已完成大约 160 课时的基础汉语学习	60—80 课时
《公务篇》	已完成大约 50 课时的基础汉语学习	60—80 课时

以上各篇均配有练习册。

该系列教程有哪些编写特点?

1. 以学习者生存需求为依据,以实用的交际任务为主线,注重听说,淡化语法。
2. 课文内容真实,语句简短易学,利于学生记忆和使用。
3. 活动形式多样,实践性强,尤其是互动性的任务活动,能够极大地增强学习者的参与意识。
4. 兼顾中国传统文化与现代生活,展示真实的中国生活图景,利于学习者融入中国社会生活。
5. 提供可灵活选用的板块和学习内容,符合短期汉语教学的特点。
6. 图文并茂,形式活泼。不但可以减轻记忆负担,还可以增加学习者的学习兴趣。
7. 利用二维码链接多种教学资源,如:录音、录音文本、课堂补充活动、课后练习和答案等。

该系列教程由中央民族大学、北京外交人员语言文化中心、北京外国语大学、南开大学等中国一流汉语教学机构的教学专家、优秀编者精心研发而成。感谢本系列教程的海内外广大使用者,感谢为该教程修订提出使用反馈意见和建议的汉语教师们!

编写组
2018 年 12 月

Preface

Since its publication in 2005, *Experiencing Chinese—Short-Term Course* has attracted the attention of tens of thousands of Chinese teachers and learners worldwide. In order to adapt to the changes over time and the rapid development of Chinese teaching, the authors of the series have conducted extensive surveys on the use of the series and carefully listened to the valuable suggestions from the top-tier teachers. With the joint efforts of the writing and editing teams, the book series has been elaborately revised and modified, and now the revised edition has been published.

What is the idea of this book series?

Following the concept of "learning language through experiencing", the book series emphasizes "learning by doing and learning by experiencing". It has designed a variety of activities throughout the courses to provide a great deal of interesting exercises, activities, games, songs, etc., so as to create a pleasant Chinese learning atmosphere and continuously stimulate students' interests in learning Chinese.

Who is this book series for?

The book series is for short-term overseas students in Chinese universities and Chinese teaching institutions, foreign diplomats and other foreigners in China. It also suits the short-term Chinese learners from Chinese teaching institutions overseas, such as Confucius Institutes, Confucius Classrooms and Chinese Language Schools, etc.

How is this book series organized?

The book series is comprised of seven volumes, which cover the main topics of short-term Chinese courses in China and overseas. The levels of difficulty and class hours of each volume are listed as follows:

Courses	Levels of Difficulty	Class Hours
Studying in China	beginners	50—70
Living in China	beginners	40—50
Living in China · Advanced	learners who have completed about 50 class hours of basic Chinese learning	60—80
Traveling in China	learners who have completed about 50 class hours of basic Chinese learning	40—50
Cultural Communication in China	learners who have completed about 160 class hours of basic Chinese learning	60—80

(to be continued)

(continued)

Courses	Levels of Difficulty	Class Hours
Business Communication in China	learners who have completed about 160 class hours of basic Chinese learning	60—80
Official Communication in China	learners who have completed about 50 class hours of basic Chinese learning	60—80

Each volume is companied by its workbook.

What makes this book series special?

1. It emphasizes listening and speaking instead of grammar, puts the learners' daily needs first, and follows practical communication tasks.
2. Its content is selected from daily life and the sentences are brief and easy to learn, which is helpful for students to memorize and use Chinese.
3. It provides various practical activities, and these interactive task-based activities can greatly enhance learners' awareness of participation.
4. It highlights both traditional Chinese culture and modern life, and reveals the real pictures of life in China, which aids the learners to blend into Chinese social life.
5. It provides a flexible selection of lively teaching modules and learning content, which is suitable for the characteristics of short-term Chinese teaching.
6. Its vivid pictures and varied activities not only relieve learners of the burden of memorization but also spark learners' interest in Chinese learning.
7. It provides a QR Code for teachers and learners, which links to a rich source of teaching materials, such as recordings, transcripts, supplementary in-class activities, after-class exercises, answers, etc.

The book series has been conscientiously written by teaching experts and excellent researchers from Minzu University of China, The Beijing Language and Cultural Center for Diplomatic Missions, Beijing Foreign Studies University, Nankai University and other top Chinese language teaching institutions in China. We sincerely give thanks to the vast number of readers in China and abroad, and to the Chinese teachers who have used this book series for teaching and have warmly provided helpful feedback and suggestions!

Authors
December 2018

使用说明

《商务篇》适用于60—80课时的汉语短期班，学生应已完成大约160课时的基础汉语学习，能用汉语进行日常交际。本书共12课，每课由"学习目标""词语""关键句式""听力任务""听力卡片""口语任务""商务任务"和"拓展"几个板块组成。学完本书，学生可掌握约210个词语及20余个关键句式。

学习目标
列出明确的学习目标，帮助师生了解当课的学习重点。

词语
采用灵活的词语展示形式，打破传统线性排列顺序，方便学生独立识认每个词语并与本课词语组合成句，满足课堂操练需要。

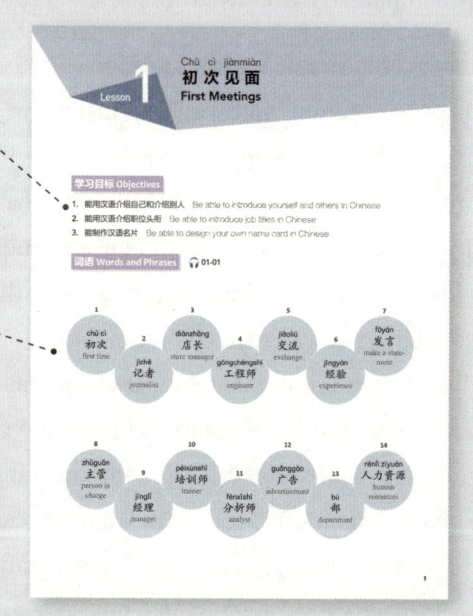

关键句式
展示本课关键句型及其使用场景与例句，并配有英文翻译，帮助学生直接掌握本课学习重点。

听力任务
包括本课主题下两个情境的听力任务，保证学生在情境中学习、在任务中学习。

任务1
与当课主题相关的机械性听力练习，帮助学生理解听力内容，夯实基础。

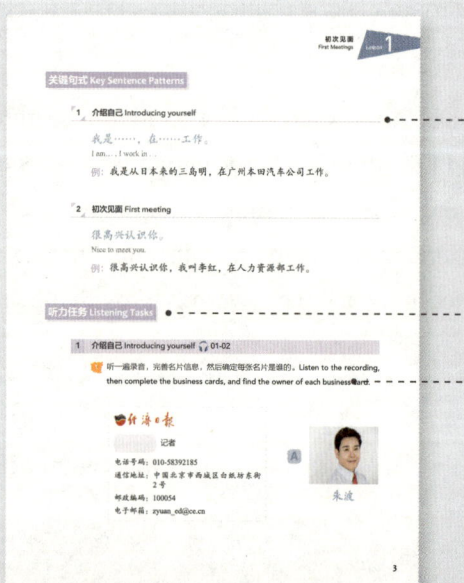

任务 2
与当课主题相关的交际性听力任务，提高学生的表达输出与口语交际能力。

听力卡片
展现听力文本，方便学生课下自学和老师课上讲解。语言简短实用，贴近日常生活，符合短期汉语教学要求。

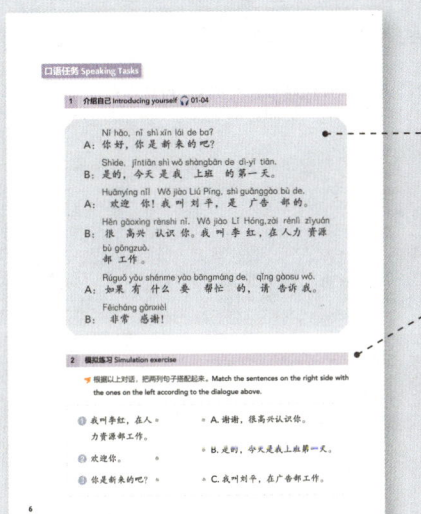

口语任务
每课包括一个真实商务活动场景下的对话，语言简短地道，适合商务汉语学习者。

模拟练习
包括课文内容或语言难点的练习。教师可在课堂上酌情选用，也可选作课后作业。

角色扮演
可用于课堂表演环节，将练习与运用相结合，调节课堂气氛，巩固所学知识。

商务体验
学生根据任务要求进行交际性练习，在实践中提高汉语运用能力。

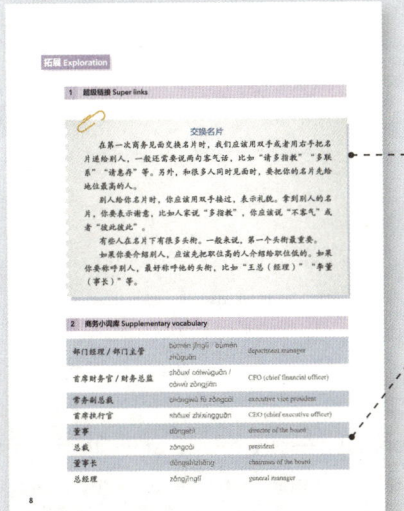

超级链接
每课提供一个与课文话题相关的知识点链接，扩充学生的相关汉语知识。

商务小词库
与每课话题相关的商务汉语常用词语，帮助学生扩展词汇量。

本册主编：张红　岳薇

2018年12月

Introduction

Business Communication in China is tailored to 60 to 80 hour-long Chinese short-term classes. Students should have already completed about 160 hours of basic Chinese learning, and should be able to use Chinese for daily communication. The book consists of 12 lessons, each lesson consisting of several sections: "Objectives" "Words and Phrases" "Key Sentences Patterns" "Listening Tasks" "Listening Cards" "Speaking Tasks" "Business Tasks" and "Exploration". Students can obtain about 210 words and more than 20 key patterns after finishing this book.

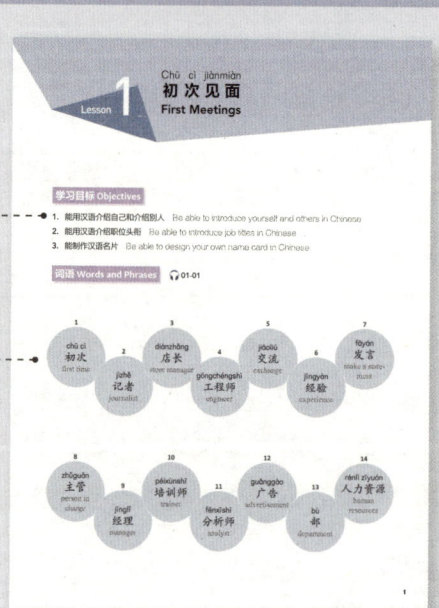

Objectives
Lists clear learning objectives, and helps teachers and students understand the key points of the lesson.

Words and Phrases
Employs a flexible method for presenting vocabulary, reorganizing the traditional linear sequence. Enables students to recognize each word independently and combine it with the other words of the lesson, to meet the needs of classroom drills.

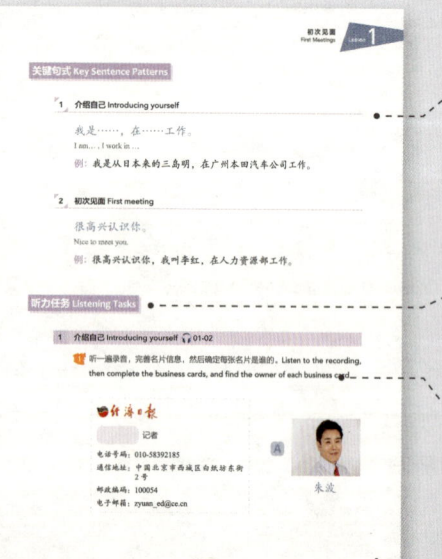

Key Sentence Patterns
Displays the key sentence patterns of this lesson, the contexts in which they are used, and examples sentences, along with English translations, so that students can directly grasp the key points of this lesson.

Listening Tasks
Includes two listening tasks related to the theme of the lesson, to ensure that students learn in context and learn through tasks.

Task 1
A mechanical exercise related to the theme of the lesson to help students understand the listening content and lay a solid foundation.

Task 2
A communicative task related to the theme of the lesson to improve students' expressive output and oral communication skills.

Listening Cards
Displays the listening text, providing aid for students to self-study and for teachers to give in-class explanations. The language is brief and practical, closely tied to daily life, and meets the requirements of short-term Chinese teaching.

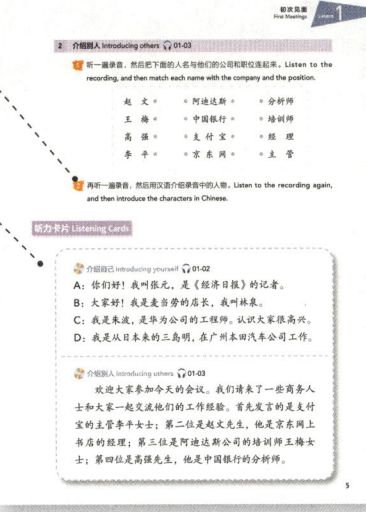

Speaking Tasks
Each lesson includes a dialogue, which features authentic activities in the business setting, and the language used is succinct and colloquial, making it suitable for business Chinese learners.

Simulation Exercise
Includes practice on the content of the texts and challenging language points. Teachers may incorporate it into classroom lessons as appropriate, or assign it as homework.

Role-play
In-class skits, combining practice and application. Switch up the classroom atmosphere, and solidify what has been learned.

Business Practice
Students conduct communicative exercises according to their tasks, and improve their ability to use Chinese in real-life situations.

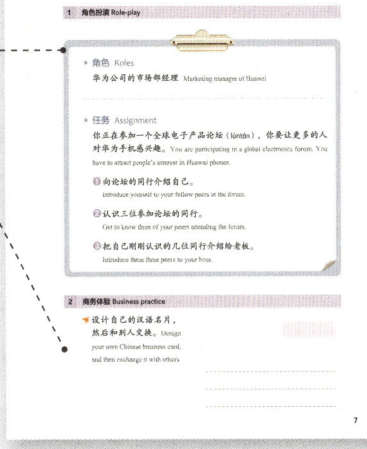

Super Links
Each lesson provides a link with knowledge points related to the topic of the lesson, to expand the learner's relevant Chinese knowledge.

Supplementary Vocabulary
Commonly used words in business Chinese, related to each topic, to help students expand their vocabulary.

Authors: Zhang Hong, Yue Wei

December 2018

目录 CONTENTS

Lesson	Objectives	Page
Lesson 1 初次见面 First Meetings	1. Be able to introduce yourself and others in Chinese 2. Be able to introduce job titles in Chinese 3. Be able to design your own name card in Chinese	1
Lesson 2 工作团队 Work Team	1. Be able to describe organizational structure of a company in Chinese 2. Be able to describe your job in Chinese 3. Be able to interview in Chinese	9
Lesson 3 日程安排 Time Schedules	1. Be able to book tickets in Chinese 2. Be able to arrange work in Chinese 3. Be able to introduce daily work in Chinese	17
Lesson 4 办公地点 Workplace Location	1. Be able to describe a company's location in Chinese 2. Be able to introduce the location of a workplace in Chinese 3. Be able to order merchandise in Chinese	25
Lesson 5 商务宴会 Business Banquet	1. Be able to arrange banquets in Chinese 2. Be able to invite guests to attend banquets in Chinese 3. Be able to give a toast in Chinese	33
Lesson 6 网上办公 Online Working	1. Be able to shop on the Chinese Internet 2. Be able to introduce online work in Chinese 3. Be able to attend a Chinese network meeting	41
Lesson 7 市场营销 Marketing	1. Be able to describe consumer behavior in Chinese 2. Be able to carry out a simple market analysis in Chinese 3. Be able to express your opinion about advertising	49

Lesson 8 财务管理 Financial Management	1. Learn about the financial management of a company 2. Be able to analyze Chinese financial statements 3. Be able to make a Chinese budget	57
Lesson 9 商业咨询 Business Consulting	1. Be able to introduce the basics of commercial consulting companies in Chinese 2. Be able to analyze the management characteristics of different companies in Chinese 3. Be able to offer consultation services to companies in Chinese	65
Lesson 10 战略管理 Strategy Management	1. Be able to describe the strategic planning process in Chinese 2. Be able to introduce how to establish a brand in Chinese 3. Be able to explain the reasons why a company changes its strategy in Chinese	73
Lesson 11 企业文化 Enterprise Culture	1. Learn about enterprise culture 2. Be able to introduce the details of enterprise culture in Chinese 3. Be able to analyze different enterprise culture in Chinese	81
Lesson 12 社会贡献 Social Contribution	1. Be able to introduce the social contributions of enterprises in Chinese 2. Be able to introduce charity activities in Chinese 3. Be able to introduce how to prepare charity activities in Chinese	89

词语表 Vocabulary Index　　97
翻译 Translation　　101

识别上方二维码
或访问 http://2d.hep.cn/51010/1
获取图书相关资源

Lesson 1

Chū cì jiànmiàn
初 次 见 面
First Meetings

学习目标 Objectives

1. 能用汉语介绍自己和介绍别人　Be able to introduce yourself and others in Chinese
2. 能用汉语介绍职位头衔　Be able to introduce job titles in Chinese
3. 能制作汉语名片　Be able to design your own name card in Chinese

词语 Words and Phrases  01-01

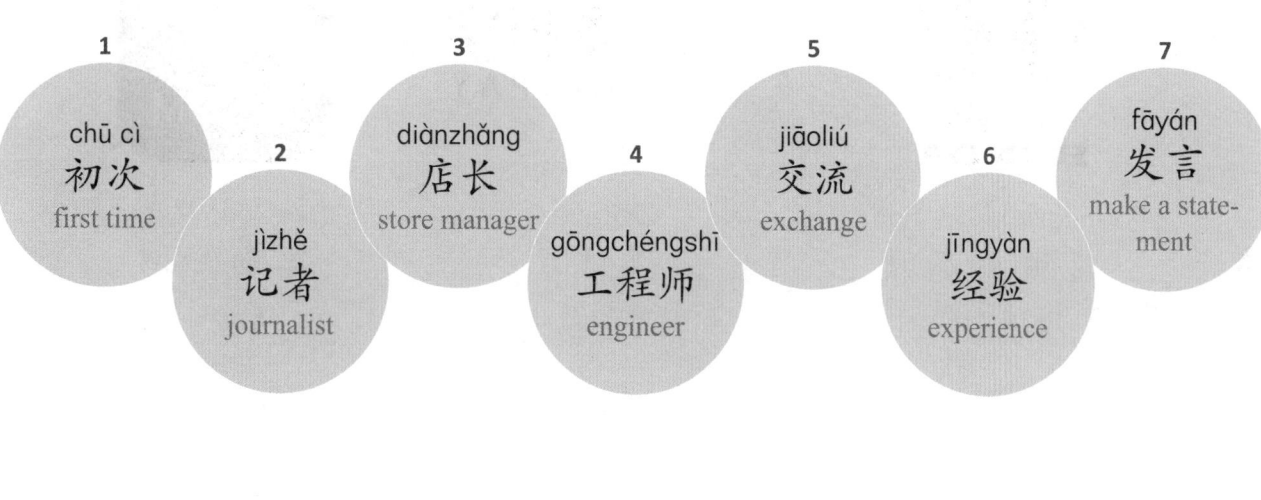

1. chū cì 初次 first time
2. jìzhě 记者 journalist
3. diànzhǎng 店长 store manager
4. gōngchéngshī 工程师 engineer
5. jiāoliú 交流 exchange
6. jīngyàn 经验 experience
7. fāyán 发言 make a statement

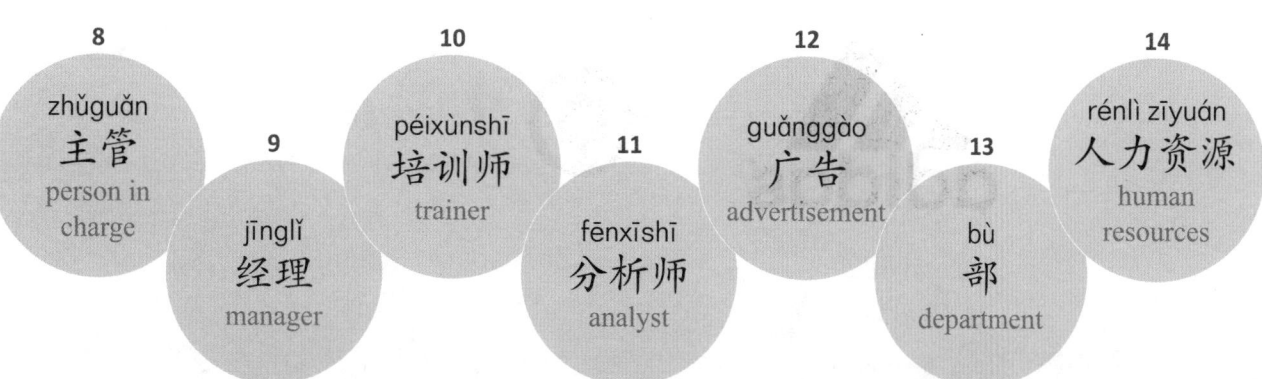

8. zhǔguǎn 主管 person in charge
9. jīnglǐ 经理 manager
10. péixùnshī 培训师 trainer
11. fēnxīshī 分析师 analyst
12. guǎnggào 广告 advertisement
13. bù 部 department
14. rénlì zīyuán 人力资源 human resources

Jīngjì Rìbào
经济 日报
Economic Daily

Màidāngláo
麦当劳
McDonald's

Huáwéi
华为
Huawei

Guǎngzhōu Běntián
广州　本田
Guangzhou Honda

Zhīfùbǎo
支付宝
Alipay

JīngDōng Wǎng
京东　网
JD.com

Ādídásī
阿迪达斯
Adidas

Zhōngguó Yínháng
中国　银行
Bank of China

初次见面 First Meetings Lesson 1

关键句式 Key Sentence Patterns

1 介绍自己 Introducing yourself

我是……，在……工作。
I am… , I work in …

例：我是从日本来的三岛明，在广州本田汽车公司工作。

2 初次见面 First meeting

很高兴认识你。
Nice to meet you.

例：很高兴认识你，我叫李红，在人力资源部工作。

听力任务 Listening Tasks

1 介绍自己 Introducing yourself 01-02

听一遍录音，完善名片信息，然后确定每张名片是谁的。Listen to the recording, then complete the business cards, and find the owner of each business card.

经济日报

  记者

电话号码：010-58392185
通信地址：中国北京市西城区白纸坊东街2号
邮政编码：100054
电子邮箱：zyuan_ed@ce.cn

朱波

林泉 _____

通信地址：中国上海市静安区南京西路1168号
邮政编码：200041
电话号码：021-52925056
电子邮箱：luckylin_job@163.com

B 三岛明

 工程师

通信地址：中国广东省深圳市龙岗区华为基地
邮政编码：100871
电话号码：0755-86941234
网址：http://www.huawei.com/cn/

C 林泉

 _____

通信地址：中国广东省广州市黄埔区广本路1号
邮政编码：510700
电话号码：020-86661661
传真号码：020-82270620
网址：http://www.ghac.cn

D 张元

2 再听一遍录音，然后选择一个人物，为他/她准备一个汉语自我介绍。Listen to the recording again, and then prepare an introduction in Chinese for one of the characters.

初次见面
First Meetings Lesson 1

2　介绍别人 Introducing others 🎧 01-03

1 听一遍录音，然后把下面的人名与他们的公司和职位连起来。Listen to the recording, and then match each name with the company and the position.

赵　文　●　　　●　阿迪达斯　●　　　●　分析师
王　梅　●　　　●　中国银行　●　　　●　培训师
高　强　●　　　●　支付宝　　●　　　●　经　理
李　平　●　　　●　京东网　　●　　　●　主　管

2 再听一遍录音，然后用汉语介绍录音中的人物。Listen to the recording again, and then introduce the characters in Chinese.

听力卡片 Listening Cards

💿 介绍自己 Introducing yourself 🎧 01-02

A：你们好！我叫张元，是《经济日报》的记者。
B：大家好！我是麦当劳的店长，我叫林泉。
C：我是朱波，是华为公司的工程师。认识大家很高兴。
D：我是从日本来的三岛明，在广州本田汽车公司工作。

💿 介绍别人 Introducing others 🎧 01-03

欢迎大家参加今天的会议。我们请来了一些商务人士和大家一起交流他们的工作经验。首先发言的是支付宝的主管李平女士；第二位是赵文先生，他是京东网上书店的经理；第三位是阿迪达斯公司的培训师王梅女士；第四位是高强先生，他是中国银行的分析师。

口语任务 Speaking Tasks

1 介绍自己 Introducing yourself 🎧 01-04

A: Nǐ hǎo, nǐ shì xīn lái de ba?
   你好，你是新来的吧？

B: Shìde, jīntiān shì wǒ shàngbān de dì-yī tiān.
   是的，今天是我上班的第一天。

A: Huānyíng nǐ! Wǒ jiào Liú Píng, shì guǎnggào bù de.
   欢迎你！我叫刘平，是广告部的。

B: Hěn gāoxìng rènshi nǐ. Wǒ jiào Lǐ Hóng, zài rénlì zīyuán bù gōngzuò.
   很高兴认识你。我叫李红，在人力资源部工作。

A: Rúguǒ yǒu shénme yào bāngmáng de, qǐng gàosu wǒ.
   如果有什么要帮忙的，请告诉我。

B: Fēicháng gǎnxiè!
   非常感谢！

2 模拟练习 Simulation exercise

根据以上对话，把两列句子搭配起来。Match the sentences on the right side with the ones on the left according to the dialogue above.

① 我叫李红，在人力资源部工作。   A. 谢谢，很高兴认识你。

② 欢迎你。   B. 是的，今天是我上班第一天。

③ 你是新来的吧？   C. 我叫刘平，在广告部工作。

初次见面 First Meetings — Lesson 1

商务任务 Business Tasks

1 角色扮演 Role-play

- **角色** Roles

  华为公司的市场部经理 Marketing manager of Huawei

- **任务** Assignment

  你正在参加一个全球电子产品论坛（lùntán），你要让更多的人对华为手机感兴趣。You are participating in a global electronics forum. You have to attract people's interest in Huawai phones.

  ❶ 向论坛的同行介绍自己。
  Introduce yourself to your fellow peers at the forum.

  ❷ 认识三位参加论坛的同行。
  Get to know three of your peers attending the forum.

  ❸ 把自己刚刚认识的几位同行介绍给老板。
  Introduce these three peers to your boss.

2 商务体验 Business practice

设计自己的汉语名片，然后和别人交换。Design your own Chinese business card, and then exchange it with others.

拓展 Exploration

1　超级链接 Super links

交换名片

在第一次商务见面交换名片时，我们应该用双手或者用右手把名片递给别人，一般还需要说两句客气话，比如"请多指教""多联系""请惠存"等。另外，和很多人同时见面时，要把你的名片先给地位最高的人。

别人给你名片时，你应该用双手接过，表示礼貌。拿到别人的名片，你要表示谢意，比如人家说"多指教"，你应该说"不客气"或者"彼此彼此"。

有些人在名片下有很多头衔。一般来说，第一个头衔最重要。

如果你要介绍别人，应该先把职位高的人介绍给职位低的。如果你要称呼别人，最好称呼他的头衔，比如"王总（经理）""李董（事长）"等。

2　商务小词库 Supplementary vocabulary

部门经理 / 部门主管	bùmén jīnglǐ / bùmén zhǔguǎn	department manager
首席财务官 / 财务总监	shǒuxí cáiwùguān / cáiwù zǒngjiān	CFO (chief financial officer)
常务副总裁	chángwù fù zǒngcái	executive vice president
首席执行官	shǒuxí zhíxíngguān	CEO (chief executive officer)
董事	dǒngshì	director of the board
总裁	zǒngcái	president
董事长	dǒngshìzhǎng	chairman of the board
总经理	zǒngjīnglǐ	general manager

Lesson 2

Gōngzuò tuánduì
工作 团队
Work Team

学习目标 Objectives

1. 能用汉语介绍公司的组织结构
   Be able to describe organizational structure of a company in Chinese
2. 能用汉语介绍工作内容　Be able to describe your job in Chinese
3. 能用汉语参加面试　Be able to interview in Chinese

词语 Words and Phrases  02-01

1. tuánduì 团队 team
2. yuángōng 员工 staff
3. bùmén 部门 department
4. yánfā 研发 research and development
5. shìchǎng 市场 market
6. chǎnpǐn 产品 product
7. yíngxiāo 营销 marketing
8. cáiwù 财务 finance
9. yùnyíng 运营 arrange
10. shēngchǎn 生产 produce
11. jīngyíng 经营 manage
12. guǎnlǐ 管理 administration
13. fùzé 负责 in charge of

14 kāifā 开发 develop
15 xiāoshòu 销售 sell
16 mìshū 秘书 secretary
17 shēnqǐng 申请 apply
18 zhíwèi 职位 position
19 lùyòng 录用 hire

Tiānmǎ Gōngsī
天马 公司
Tianma Company

Běijīng Dàxué
北京 大学
Peking University

关键句式 Key Sentence Patterns

1 介绍公司部门 Introducing the departments of a company

公司有……：一个是……，一个是……，还有一个是……
The company has... : one is... , one is... , and there's also...

例： 公司有4个部门：一个是研发部，一个是市场部，一个是财务部，还有一个是运营部。

工作团队 Work Team — Lesson 2

2　介绍工作内容 Describing responsibilities

负责……（工作）
in charge of...

例：天马公司的总经理全面负责公司的经营活动。

3　应聘工作 Applying for a job

1）申请……（职位）
apply for... (position)

例：你为什么申请营销部的职位?

2）有……年……的经验
have... years of experience in...

例：我有五年市场营销的经验。

听力任务 Listening Tasks

1　介绍公司部门 Introducing the departments of a company 🎧 02-02

听一遍录音，然后圈出天马公司的部门。Listen to the recording, and then circle the departments that are in the Tianma Company.

① 研发部
② 技术部
③ 运营部
④ 营销部
⑤ 财务部
⑥ 人力资源部

2 再听一遍录音，然后完成下面的句子，并用汉语介绍一下天马公司。Listen to the recording again, and then complete the sentences below and introduce the Tianma Company in Chinese.

① 天马公司一共有_____名员工，有_____个部门。

② 天马公司的_____是绿色食品。

2 介绍工作内容 Describing responsibilities 🎧 02-03

1 听一遍录音，然后填空，并把下面的职位与相应的工作内容连起来。Listen to the recording, then fill in the blanks and match the position with the job content.

职位	工作内容
_____经理 •	• 产品销售
_____经理 •	• 新产品开发、生产管理
_____经理 •	• 公司的经营
_____经理 •	• 人力资源管理
总经理_____ •	• 财务工作

2 再听一遍录音，然后用汉语介绍天马公司的组织结构。Listen to the recording again, and then introduce the organizational structure of the Tianma Company in Chinese.

工作团队 Work Team　Lesson 2

听力卡片 Listening Cards

介绍公司部门 Introducing the departments of a company 🎧 02-02

天马公司是一家新公司，一共有 20 名员工，公司有 4 个部门，一个是研发部，一个是营销部，一个是财务部，还有一个是运营部。公司的产品是绿色食品。

介绍工作内容 Describing responsibilities 🎧 02-03

天马公司的总经理负责公司的经营活动，研发生产经理负责新产品的开发、生产管理，市场营销经理负责市场开发和产品销售，财务经理负责财务工作，总经理秘书负责管理运营、人力资源等工作。

口语任务 Speaking Tasks

1　面试 A job interview 🎧 02-04

Miànshìguān: Qǐng tántan nǐ de qíngkuàng ba.
面试官：请 谈谈 你的 情况 吧。

Yìngpìnzhě: Wǒ èr líng yī líng nián cóng Běijīng Dàxué bìyè,
应聘者：我 2010 年 从 北京 大学 毕业,
zài yì jiā diànnǎo gōngsī gōngzuòle sān nián.
在 一家 电脑 公司 工作了 三 年。

Miànshìguān: Nǐ wèi shénme shēnqǐng yíngxiāobù jīnglǐ
面试官：你 为 什么 申请 营销部 经理
zhíwèi?
职位？

13

Yìngpìnzhě: Yīnwèi wǒ yǒu wǔ nián shìchǎng yíngxiāo de jīngyàn.
应聘者：因为我有五年市场营销的经验。

Miànshìguān: Rúguǒ wǒmen lùyòng nǐ, nǐ shénme shíhou néng shàngbān?
面试官：如果我们录用你，你什么时候能上班？

Yìngpìnzhě: Wǒ kěyǐ mǎshàng gōngzuò.
应聘者：我可以马上工作。

2 模拟练习 Simulation exercise

根据以上对话，完成对话。Complete the dialogues according to the dialogue above.

❶ A：_____？ B：我在一家电脑公司工作了三年。

❷ A：你想申请什么职位？ B：_____。

❸ A：你什么时候能上班？ B：_____。

商务任务 Business Tasks

1 角色扮演 Role-play

• 角色 Roles

A：你 You
B：朋友 Your friend

工作团队
Work Team
Lesson 2

• **任务** Assignment

你和朋友准备开一家互联网公司，用汉语讨论一下你们要设置哪些部门，分别负责什么工作。

You are starting an Internet company with a friend. Discuss what departments you need to set up, and their responsibilities in Chinese.

2 商务体验 Business practices

填写应聘表。Fill out the application form in Chinese.

姓　　名		性　别	
国　　籍			
出生年月			
学　　历		专　业	
毕业学校			
工作经历			
申请职位			
地　　址			
联系方式			

拓展 Exploration

1　超级链接 Super links

小米科技的管理模式

　　小米科技公司崇尚创新、快速的互联网文化,主张让每位员工在轻松的伙伴式工作氛围中发挥自己的创意。提到小米团队,不得不提到小米扁平化的管理模式:产品、营销、硬件、电商,每个领域由一名创始人坐镇,直接领导员工,各个领域之间互不干涉,一起把自己负责的领域做得更好。这样的管理制度可以保证信息的传递速度,使高层快速发现信息所反映的真实问题,并及时做出决策;同时,也大大提高了团队的反应能力和协调能力,员工的主动性和首创精神也得到了极大激发,从而提高了团队的工作效率。

2　商务小词库 Supplementary vocabulary

层级	céngjí	hierarchy
企业家	qǐyèjiā	entrepreneur
董事会	dǒngshìhuì	board of directors
提升	tíshēng	promote
公关部	gōngguān bù	public relations department
职业	zhíyè	occupation
简历	jiǎnlì	resume
组织结构	zǔzhī jiégòu	organizational structure

Lesson 3

Rìchéng ānpái
日程 安排
Time Schedules

学习目标 Objectives

1. 能用汉语预订机票　Be able to book tickets in Chinese
2. 能用汉语安排工作　Be able to arrange work in Chinese
3. 能用汉语介绍日常工作　Be able to introduce daily work in Chinese

词语 Words and Phrases  03-01

1. rìchéng 日程 schedule
2. ānpái 安排 arrangement
3. yùdìng 预订 book; reserve
4. wǎngfǎn piào 往返票 round-trip ticket
5. jīngjì cāng 经济舱 economy class
6. gōngwù cāng 公务舱 business class
7. qǐyè 企业 enterprise
8. zǒngjié 总结 summary
9. gōngchǎng 工厂 factory
10. chákàn 查看 check
11. gōutōng 沟通 communicate
12. chējiān 车间 workshop (in a factory)
13. kèhù 客户 customer

Zhōngguó Guójì Hángkōng Gōngsī (Guó Háng)
中国 国际 航空 公司（国 航）
Air China

Dōngjīng
东京
Tokyo

关键句式 Key Sentence Patterns

1 预订机票 Booking a ticket

我要预订……月……号从……到……的机票。
I want to book a flight from... to... (place) on... (date).

例：我要预订3张5月25号从北京到东京的机票。

2 安排工作 Arranging work

1）上午……下午……（最后……）

In the morning... , in the afternoon... (finally...)

例：第一天上午参观公司，下午学习企业文化，晚上参加团队活动，最后对这次培训进行总结。

2）先……，然后……

First... , and then...

例：我先查一下电子邮件，然后了解前一天的生产情况。

日程安排
Time Schedules   Lesson 3

听力任务 Listening Tasks

1　预订机票 Booking a ticket 🎧 03-02

1 听一遍录音，然后填空。Listen to the recording, and then fill in the blanks.

_____月_____日　✈　从_____到_____
_____月_____日　✈　从_____到_____

2 再听一遍录音，然后用汉语介绍机票预订的情况。Listen to the recording again, and then introduce the flight reservation in Chinese.

2　安排工作 Arranging work 🎧 03-03

1 听一遍录音，然后按照时间顺序给王梅两天的培训活动排序。Listen to the recording, and then sort out Wang Mei's training activities.

○ 介绍企业文化

○ 和新员工交流

○ 组织团队活动

○ 总结　　○ 带新员工参观

2 再听一遍录音，然后用汉语介绍王梅的培训活动。Listen to the recording again, and then introduce Wang Mei's training activities in Chinese.

19

听力卡片 Listening Cards

🔘 预订机票 Booking a ticket 🎧 03-02

国航预订：您好，请问有什么可以帮您？

公司秘书：我要预订3张5月25号从北京到东京的机票。

国航预订：好的，请问您是订往返票吗？

公司秘书：对，订往返票。回北京的时间是6月1号。

国航预订：好的。请问您需要经济舱还是公务舱？

公司秘书：1张经济舱，2张公务舱。

国航预订：下午3点的飞机可以吗？

公司秘书：可以。

🔘 安排工作 Arranging work 🎧 03-03

王梅是阿迪达斯北京公司的一名培训师，她经常为员工做培训。上个星期，王梅组织了两天的新员工培训。

第一天上午，王梅帮助新员工了解了企业文化，下午和晚上组织了各种团队活动；第二天上午，王梅带新员工参观了公司管理部门；下午，王梅继续和新员工交流；最后对这两天的培训做了总结。

日程安排 Time Schedules — Lesson 3

口语任务 Speaking Tasks

1 日常工作 Daily work 🎧 03-04

Jìzhě: Qǐng tántan nín de rìcháng gōngzuò, hǎo ma?
记者：请 谈谈 您的 日常 工作，好吗？

Sāndǎo Míng: Wǒ yìbān bā diǎn dào gōngchǎng, xiān chákàn yóuxiāng, chǔlǐ yóujiàn, ránhòu liǎojiě qián yì tiān de shēngchǎn qíngkuàng.
三岛 明：我 一般 8 点 到 工厂，先 查看 邮箱，处理 邮件，然后 了解 前 一 天 的 生产 情况。

Jìzhě: Nín hé qítā jīnglǐ zěnme gōutōng ne?
记者：您 和 其他 经理 怎么 沟通 呢？

Sāndǎo Míng: Wǒmen měi tiān shàngwǔ kāi yí cì gōutōng huì.
三岛 明：我们 每天 上午 开一次 沟通 会。

Jìzhě: Xiàwǔ ne?
记者：下午 呢？

Sāndǎo Míng: Xiàwǔ jīngcháng zài shēngchǎn chējiān.
三岛 明：下午 经常 在 生产 车间。

Jìzhě: Nín yìbān shénme shíhou xiàbān ne?
记者：您 一般 什么 时候 下班 呢？

Sāndǎo Míng: Liù diǎn zuǒyòu ba, búguò yǒushíhou yào jiàn yìxiē kèhù.
三岛 明：6 点 左右 吧，不过 有时候 要 见 一些 客户。

2　模拟练习 Simulation exercise

根据以上对话，补充三岛明的活动，然后把时间与相应的活动连起来。Complete Sandao Ming's schedule according to the dialogue above, and then match the work with the time.

和其他经理开会_____

在生产_____

下班或见客户_____

_____前一天的生产情况

_____电子邮箱

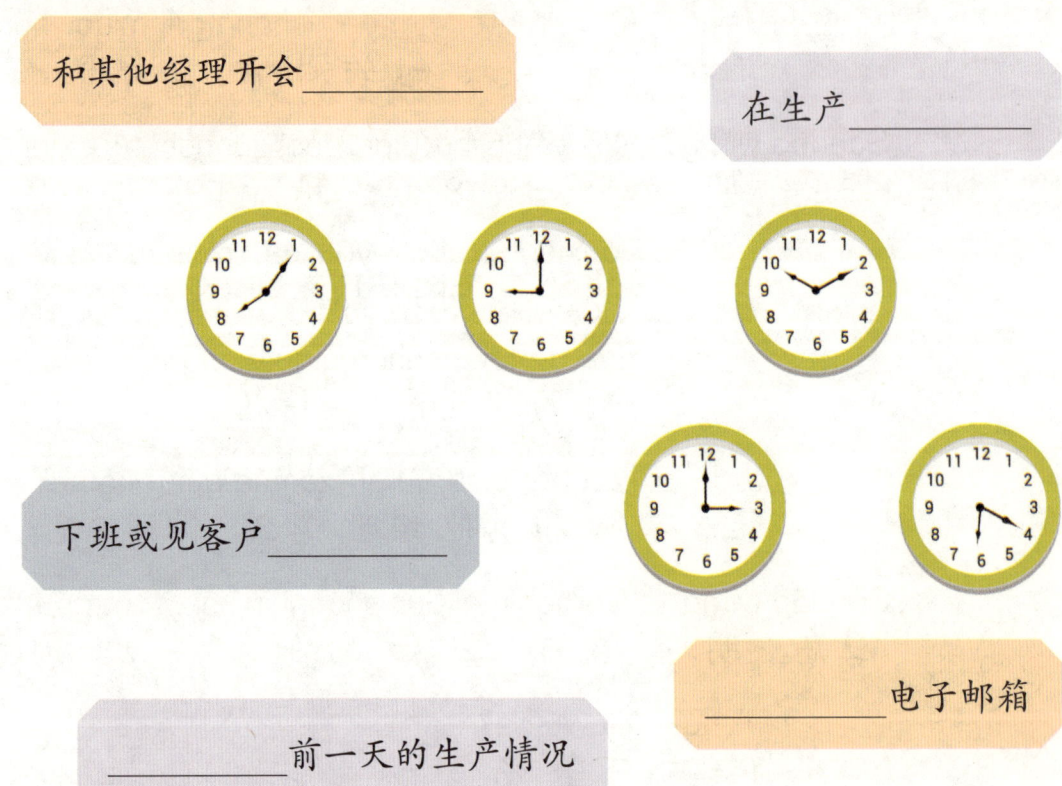

商务任务 Business Tasks

1　角色扮演 Role-play

- **角色 Roles**

    A：销售经理　Sales manager
    B：研发经理　Development manager

日程安排
Time Schedules Lesson 3

• **任务** Assignment

请根据日程确定员工身份，然后选择一个角色说说自己的日常工作。Identify the staff's position according to the schedules, then select a role and talk about your daily work.

日程 A

8:30 到公司，先查电子邮箱

9:00 给客户打电话

13:00 与其他经理沟通销售情况

19:00 参加商务活动

日程 B

9:00 到公司

10:00 与其他员工讨论产品设计

15:00 去工厂的生产车间

19:00 下班

2 商务体验 Business practice

请根据下面的活动安排你的日程。Use the following activities to arrange a personal schedule.

2019年3月10号9:00在上海参加交流会，3月12号上午10:00在北京接待客户，期间有以下几件事需要做：

✓ 参观一家中国公司

✓ 参观你们公司在上海的工厂

✓ 与客户见面并一起用餐

✓ 与公司一些经理开会

✓ 游览上海

✓ 看朋友

拓展 Exploration

1　超级链接 Super links

注重个人和团队的共同力量

　　格力公司不仅希望员工拥有良好的个人素质,更希望员工们能融入团队,互帮互助,共同进步。

　　格力公司鼓励员工积极参与团队会议,并在团队会议中发言,公司对踊跃发言的员工会给以奖励和表扬。公司还经常组织团队活动,以此培养员工的团结合作精神。

　　团队的力量是无穷的。格力公司正是想要通过这些活动,帮助员工树立集体意识,充分发挥自身优势,为团队做出宝贵的贡献。

2　商务小词库 Supplementary vocabulary

传真	chuánzhēn	fax
度假	dùjià	take a vocation
单程票	dānchéng piào	one-way ticket
留言	liúyán	leave a message
登机	dēngjī	board a plane
手续	shǒuxù	procedure
电子机票	diànzǐ jīpiào	e-ticket
运动设施	yùndòng shèshī	sport facilities

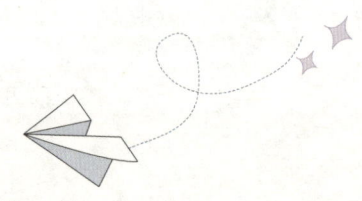

Lesson 4

Bàngōng dìdiǎn
办公 地点
Workplace Location

学习目标 Objectives

1. 能用汉语描述公司位置　Be able to describe a company's location in Chinese
2. 能用汉语介绍工作地点　Be able to introduce the location of a workplace in Chinese
3. 能用汉语订购商品　Be able to order merchandise in Chinese

词语 Words and Phrases  04-01

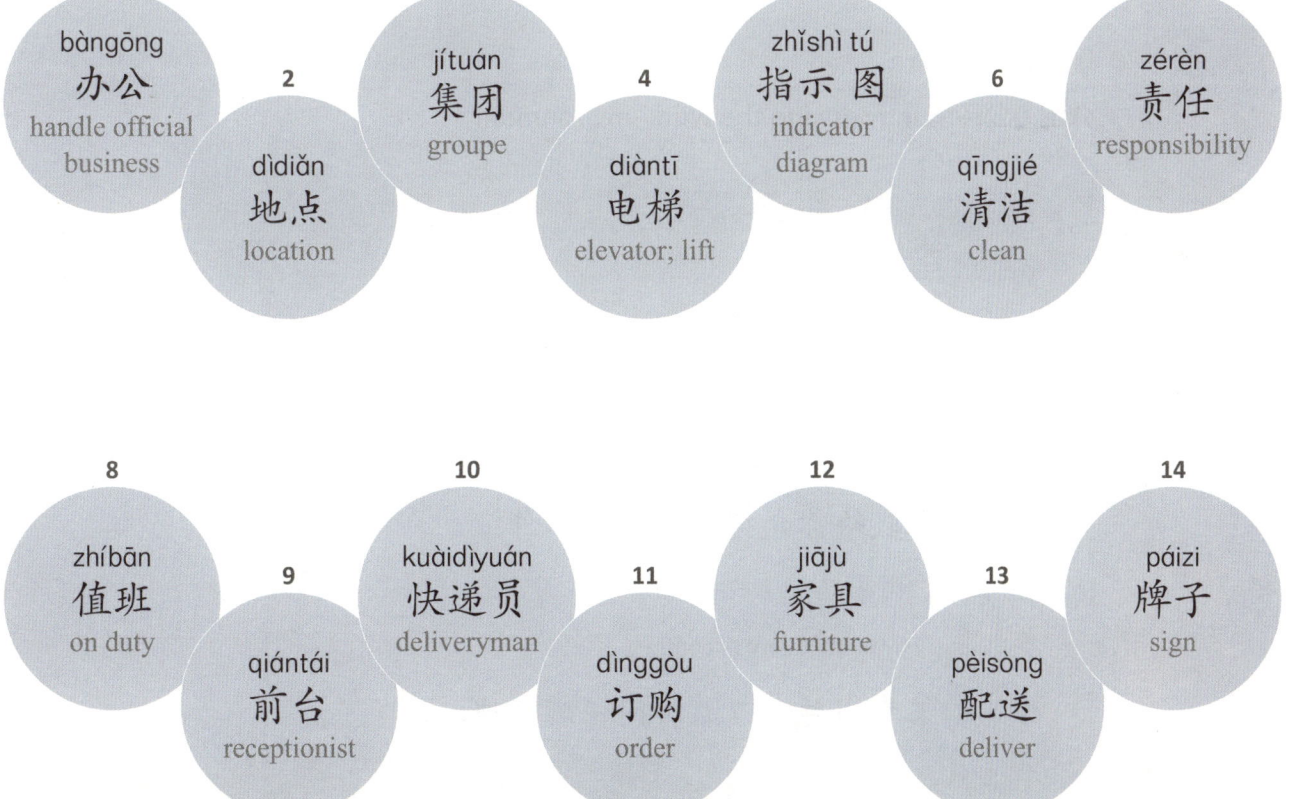

1. bàngōng 办公 handle official business
2. dìdiǎn 地点 location
3. jítuán 集团 groupe
4. diàntī 电梯 elevator; lift
5. zhǐshì tú 指示图 indicator diagram
6. qīngjié 清洁 clean
7. zérèn 责任 responsibility
8. zhíbān 值班 on duty
9. qiántái 前台 receptionist
10. kuàidìyuán 快递员 deliveryman
11. dìnggòu 订购 order
12. jiājù 家具 furniture
13. pèisòng 配送 deliver
14. páizi 牌子 sign

Shùnfēng Sùyùn
顺丰 速运
SF Express

关键句式 Key Sentence Patterns

1 介绍公司环境 Introducing a company's environment

……大楼/……部/……公司在……
... Building / ... Department / ... Company is at / in

例：公司的人力资源部在 7 层 706 房间。

2 介绍办公环境 Introducing the work environment

1）欢迎……来到……
Welcome to...

例：欢迎你来到麦当劳工作。

2）现在我给你介绍……
Now let me introduce... to you.

例：现在我给你介绍一下你的工作。

3）如果有问题可以……
You can... if you have any problem.

例：如果有问题可以随时问值班经理。

办公地点
Workplace Location
Lesson 4

听力任务 Listening Tasks

1　介绍公司环境 Introducing company's environment 🎧 04-02

1 听一遍录音，然后填空。Listen to the recording, and then fill in the blanks.

方正集团大楼在_____，共有_____层，大楼共有_____电梯。大楼的一层有全楼的_____，_____在大楼的_____层和3层，公司的人力资源部在_____房间，财务部在_____房间。

2 再听一遍录音，然后用汉语介绍方正集团大楼。Listen to the recording again, and then introduce the Founder Building in Chinese.

2　介绍办公环境 Introducing the work environment 🎧 04-03

1 听一遍录音，然后填空。Listen to the recording, and then fill in the blanks.

单　　位：_____

工作时间：_____到_____，中间休息_____

负　　责：_____工作

27

2 再听一遍录音，然后用汉语介绍麦当劳的工作。Listen to the recording again, and then introduce the McDonald's work activities in Chinese.

听力卡片 Listening Cards

🎧 **介绍公司环境** Introducing a company's environment 04-02

方正集团大楼在北京市的西北边，大楼一共有18层，大楼有两部电梯，大楼的一层有全楼的指示图。方正集团销售部在方正集团大楼的2层和3层。公司的人力资源部在7层706房间，财务部在8层808房间。

🎧 **介绍办公环境** Introducing the work environment 04-03

欢迎你来到麦当劳工作。我是这个店的店长。现在我给你介绍一下你的工作。你的上班时间是下午两点半到晚上十一点，要至少提前十五分钟到店。中间有半个小时的休息时间。你负责2层的清洁工作，如果有人需要帮助，你有责任去帮助他们。如果有问题可以随时问值班经理。

办公地点
Workplace Location Lesson 4

口语任务 Speaking Tasks

1 公司地址 Company's location 🎧 04-04

Qiántái: Nǐ hǎo! Tiānmǎ Gōngsī.
前台：你好！天马公司。

Kuàidìyuán: Nǐ hǎo! Wǒ shì Shùnfēng Sùyùn de kuàidìyuán,
快递员：你好！我是顺丰速运的快递员，
nín dìnggòu de bàngōng jiājù dào le, wǒmen
您订购的办公家具到了，我们
xiànzài zhèngzài ānpái pèisòng. Qǐng wèn, sòng
现在正在安排配送。请问，送
dào nǎli bǐjiào fāngbiàn?
到哪里比较方便？

Qiántái: Nǐ dào Běijīng Dàxué xīnán mén, kànjiàn pángbiān
前台：你到北京大学西南门，看见旁边
yǒu yì jiā Zhōngguó Yínháng, wǒmen gōngsī jiù
有一家中国银行，我们公司就
zài tā de duìmiàn, ménkǒu yǒu wǒmen gōngsī de
在它的对面，门口有我们公司的
páizi.
牌子。

Kuàidìyuán: Hǎode. Běijīng Dàxué xīnán mén pángbiān
快递员：好的。北京大学西南门旁边
Zhōngguó Yínháng de duìmiàn.
中国银行的对面。

Qiántái: Méi cuò, yǒu wèntí kěyǐ zài dǎ diànhuà.
前台：没错，有问题可以再打电话。

Kuàidìyuán: Xièxie! Zàijiàn.
快递员：谢谢！再见。

2 模拟练习 Simulation exercise

1 根据前页对话,画出天马公司的位置。Mark the location of the Tianma Company according to the dialogue on the previous page.

2 根据前页对话,完成下面的句子,然后用汉语介绍天马公司的位置。Complete the sentences according to the dialogue on the previons page, and then introduce the Tianma Company location in Chinese.

_____大学_____门旁边有一家_____,天马公司在中国银行的_____。

办公地点
WORKPLACE LOCATION   Lesson 4

商务任务 Business Tasks

1 角色扮演 Role-play

- **角色** Roles
  - A：小米科技公司办公室秘书 Xiaomi Tech office secretary
  - B：办公用品超市员工 Office Supermarket Staff

- **任务** Assignment

给办公用品超市打电话订购下列办公用品。Call the Office Supermarket and order the office supplies listed below.

名称 Name of Commodity	椅子	书架	会议桌
货号 Code Number	C1138063	D1558792	M937115
数量 Quantity	600 把	30 个	18 张

2 商务体验 Business practice

给麦当劳打电话，为办公室同事预订 3 份套餐，并告诉快递员公司地点。Call McDonald's and order three set meals, and tell the deliveryman your company's location.

31

拓展 Exploration

1　超级链接 Super links

快递在中国

随着网络购物的普及，快递业在中国越来越发达。小到一双袜子，大到一台电冰箱都可以通过快递运送。有了快递，在北京也可以吃到新鲜的新疆葡萄、美味的江苏大闸蟹……不管刮风下雨，每天你都可以看到很多快递员在街道上穿梭，这也为中国人带来了更多的就业机会。同时，快递也催生了很多其他行业，网上药店、网上花店、网上饭店等层出不穷。总之，快递让中国人的生活更方便了。

2　商务小词库 Supplementary vocabulary

保险柜	bǎoxiǎnguì	safe (n.)
耗材	hàocái	consumables
保修期	bǎoxiūqī	warranty period
快件	kuàijiàn	express mail
打印机	dǎyìnjī	printer
数码	shùmǎ	digital
复印机	fùyìnjī	copy machine
投影仪	tóuyǐngyí	projector

Lesson 5

Shāngwù yànhuì
商务 宴会
Business Banquet

学习目标 Objectives

1. 能用汉语安排宴会　Be able to arrange banquets in Chinese
2. 能用汉语邀请客人参加宴会　Be able to invite guests to attend banquets in Chinese
3. 能用汉语祝酒　Be able to give a toast in Chinese

词语 Words and Phrases  05-01

1. yànhuì 宴会 banquet
2. jiǔdiàn 酒店 hotel
3. suíyì 随意 feel free to
4. jǔbàn 举办 hold
5. huàláng 画廊 gallery
6. hézuò 合作 coorporation
7. yúkuài 愉快 pleasant
8. tóngshì 同事 colleague
9. qìngzhù 庆祝 celebrate
10. hézuòshāng 合作商 official partner
11. zhìliàng 质量 quality
12. hélǐ 合理 reasonable
13. jìnkǒu 进口 import
14. chénggōng 成功 successful
15. gānbēi 干杯 cheers

33

Běihǎi Gōngyuán
北海 公园
Beihai Park

Běijīng Fàndiàn
北京 饭店
Beijing Hotel

Wángfǔjǐng
王府井
Wangfujing

Quánjùdé Kǎoyā Diàn
全聚德 烤鸭 店
Quanjude Roast Duck Restaurant

关键句式 Key Sentence Patterns

1 安排宴会 Arranging a banquet

1) 商务宴会已经安排好了。

   The business banquet has been arranged.

2) 在……举办商务宴会。

   The business banquet is held at/in...

   例：现在人们可以在公园举办商务宴会。

2 宴会祝酒 Toasting on a banquet

1) 我们这次合作得非常愉快。

   We collaborated happily this time.

2) 为了庆祝我们合作成功，干杯！

   Let's have a toast to celebrate our successful collaboration.

商务宴会
Business Banquet Lesson 5

听力任务 Listening Tasks

1 安排宴会 Arranging a banquet 🎧 05-02

1 听一遍录音，然后完成下表。Listen to the recording, and then fill in the table below.

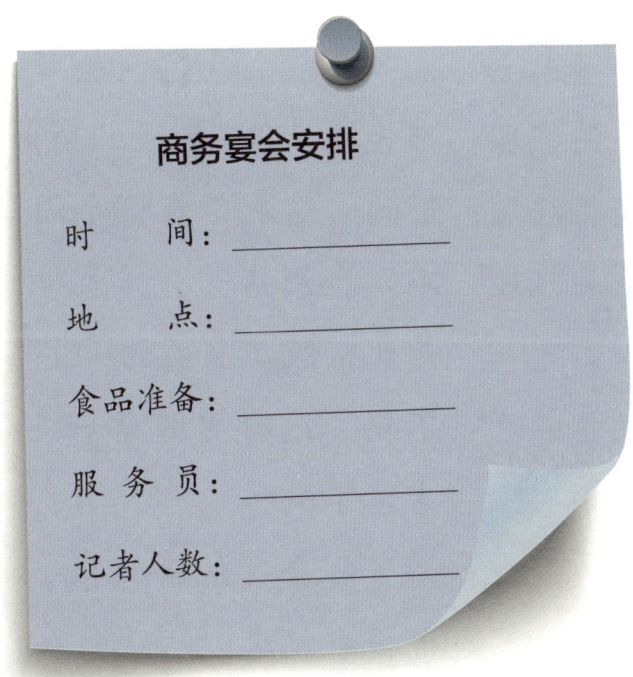

商务宴会安排

时　　间：_____

地　　点：_____

食品准备：_____

服 务 员：_____

记者人数：_____

2 再听一遍录音，然后用汉语介绍宴会安排。Listen to the recording again, and then introduce the banquet arrangements in Chinese.

2 商务宴会 Business banquet 🎧 05-03

1 听一遍录音，然后圈出饭店的工作。Listen to the recording, and then circle the hotel's responsibilities.

准备食品　　　　　　选择宴会地点

让服务员来服务　　　给客人打电话

35

2 再听一遍录音，然后用汉语介绍商务宴会的准备工作。Listen to the recording again, and then introduce the preparation required for a business banquet in Chinese.

听力卡片 Listening Cards

安排宴会 Arranging a banquet 🎧 05-02

公关经理：张经理，下星期五的商务宴会已经安排好了。

销售经理：好的，这次是在哪个酒店？

公关经理：不是在酒店里，是在北海公园。不过，食品是北京饭店准备的，服务员也是北京饭店的。

销售经理：不错。这样更随意一些。《经济日报》的记者请了吗？

公关经理：请了一个《经济日报》的记者，还请了一个电视台记者。

销售经理：太好了！

商务宴会 Business banquet 🎧 05-03

商务宴会常常在哪里举办？很多人的回答都是"在酒店里"。其实现在人们也可以在公园或者画廊举办商务宴会，这样可以更随意一些。你选好了地点，给酒店的宴会销售部打电话，他们就会帮你安排好一切。比如一家公司决定在北海公园举办宴会，酒店就会做好各种准备，所有食品和服务都和在酒店里一样，酒店的服务员也会来服务。

商务宴会 Business Banquet Lesson 5

口语任务 Speaking Tasks

1 商务宴会 Business banquet 🎧 05-04

Xiāoshòu jīnglǐ: Wǒmen zhè cì hézuò de fēicháng yúkuài, wǒ
销售 经理： 我们 这次 合作 得 非常 愉快，我
xiǎng qǐng nín hé nín de tóngshì yìqǐ chī
想 请 您 和 您 的 同事 一起 吃
wǎnfàn, qìngzhù yí xià.
晚饭， 庆祝 一下。

Hézuòshāng: Xièxie. Wǒmen yě hěn gāoxìng hé nín hézuò.
合作商： 谢谢。 我们 也 很 高兴 和 您 合作。

Xiāoshòu jīnglǐ: Míngtiān wǎnshang qī diǎn wǒ zài Wángfǔjǐng
销售 经理： 明天 晚上 7 点 我 在 王府井
de Quánjùdé Kǎoyā Diàn ménkǒu děng nǐmen,
的 全聚德 烤鸭 店 门口 等 你们，
hǎo ma?
好 吗？

Hézuòshāng: Hǎode, wǒmen dōu hěn xǐhuān kǎoyā. Nà
合作商： 好的， 我们 都 很 喜欢 烤鸭。那
wǒmen míng wǎn qī diǎn jiàn!
我们 明 晚 7 点 见！

（At the banquet）

Hézuòshāng： Nǐmen de dàyī zhìliàng hǎo, jiàgé yě hélǐ,
合作商： 你们 的 大衣 质量 好，价格 也 合理，
xià cì wǒmen yào duō jìnkǒu yíwàn jiàn.
下次 我们 要 多 进口 10000 件。

Xiāoshòu jīnglǐ： Zhè zhǒng dàyī zài guónèi xiāoshòu de yě
销售 经理： 这 种 大衣 在 国内 销售 得 也
fēicháng hǎo. Wèile qìngzhù wǒmen hézuò
非常 好。 为了 庆祝 我们 合作
chénggōng, gānbēi!
成功， 干杯！

Hézuòshāng： Yě wèi jīnhòu de hézuò, gānbēi!
合作商： 也 为 今后 的 合作，干杯！

2　模拟练习 Simulation exercise

1 选词填空。Fill in the blanks with the proper words.

进口　　　同事　　　成功

① 我想请您和您_____一起吃晚饭。

② 为了庆祝我们合作_____，干杯！

③ 下次我们要多_____10000件大衣。

2 完成对话。Complete the dialogues.

① A：我们很高兴和您合作！

　 B：_____！

商务宴会　Business Banquet　Lesson 5

❷ A：这种大衣销售得怎么样？

　　B：_____。

商务任务 Business Tasks

1　角色扮演 Role-play

• **角色** Roles
　A：东风汽车公司销售经理 Dongfeng Motor Corporation sales manager
　B：汽车进口商 Automobile import seller

• **任务** Assignment
在商务宴会上庆祝合作成功。Celebrate their successful collaboration at a business banquet.

2　商务体验 Business practice

➤ 下个星期三，你的公司要在朝阳公园举办商务宴会，请你给香格里拉酒店的宴会销售部打电话预订。Your company will hold a business banquet in Chaoyang Park next Wednesday. Call the Shangri-La Hotel Banquet Marketing Department to make a reservation.

拓展 Exploration

1　超级链接 Super links

商务宴会常用的祝酒词

★ 各位先生、女士，晚上好！首先请允许我代表我们公司全体员工，对大家的到来表示诚挚的感谢和问候。

★ 我谨代表公司向出席今天晚宴的各位领导、各位来宾和各位朋友，表示衷心的感谢并致以诚挚的敬意！

★ 感谢各位在百忙之中能够抽空来参加我们公司的宴会。

★ 祝大家工作顺利、身体健康、万事如意，干杯！

★ 最后，为我们之间正式建立友好合作关系，为今后我们之间的密切合作，干杯！

2　商务小词库 Supplementary vocabulary

观摩团	guānmó tuán	visiting group
贵宾	guìbīn	honored guest
宴请	yànqǐng	entertain (to dinner)
出席	chūxí	present (at a banquet, etc.)
品茶	pǐn chá	tea tasting
祝酒	zhùjiǔ	toast
答谢宴会	dáxiè yànhuì	return banquet
宴会厅	yànhuì tīng	banquet hall

Lesson 6

Wǎngshàng bàngōng
网上 办公
Online Working

学习目标 Objectives

1. 能在汉语网站购物　Be able to shop on the Chinese Internet
2. 能用汉语介绍网上办公　Be able to introduce online work in Chinese
3. 能用汉语参加网络会议　Be able to attend a Chinese network meeting

词语 Words and Phrases 06-01

1. zhékòu 折扣 discount
2. guòchéng 过程 process
3. wǎngzhàn 网站 website
4. dìzhǐ 地址 address
5. fùkuǎn 付款 pay
6. tíjiāo 提交 submit
7. xìnxī dān 信息单 information sheet
8. tígōng 提供 provide
9. miǎnfèi 免费 free
10. diànzǐ bǎn 电子版 electronic edition
11. shàngchuán 上传 upload
12. hùliánwǎng 互联网 Internet
13. ruǎnjiàn 软件 software
14. tōngzhī 通知 notice
15. liánxì 联系 contact

Qǐyè Wēixìn
企业 微信
WeChat Work

Niǔyuē
纽约
New York City

关键句式 Key Sentence Patterns

1　网上购物 Online shopping

先……，然后……，就可以……
First... , then... , and you can ...

例：你先找到想要的书，填写信息单，然后提交，几天以后，你就可以收到书了。

2　网上办公 Online working

……离不开……
... cannot... without...

例：我每天的工作都离不开互联网。

3　网络会议 Online meeting

你们听得清楚吗?
Can you hear clearly?

网上办公
Online Working   Lesson 6

听力任务 Listening Tasks

1　网上购物 Online shopping 🎧 06-02

① 听一遍录音，然后填空。Listen to the recording, and then fill in the blanks.

① 京东网是中国有名的_____书店。

② 在京东网买书一般都有一些_____。

③ 在京东网买书，你先_____，填写信息单，然后_____，几天以后，你就可以收到书了。

④ 如果买的多，网站还提供_____。

② 再听一遍录音，然后用汉语介绍如何在网上买书。Listen to the recording again, and then introduce how to purchase books online in Chinese.

2　网上办公 Online working 🎧 06-03

① 听一遍录音，然后填空。Listen to the recording, and then fill in the blanks.

① 分析师每天_____电子邮件。

② 《经济日报》几年前就有了_____。

③ 老师讲课的内容可以_____到互联网上。

④ 经理可以用网上办公软件_____。

② 再听一遍录音，然后用汉语说说在互联网上可以完成哪些工作。Listen to the recording again, and then talk about the works can be finished on the Internet in Chinese.

43

听力卡片 Listening Cards

🔘 网上购物 Online shopping 🎧 06-02

京东网是中国有名的网上书店,在京东网,你可以买到自己喜欢的纸质书、电子书和CD等。京东网买书一般都有些折扣,过程也很简单。进入网站,你先找到想要的书,填写你的地址、电话和付款方式,然后提交信息单,几天之后你就可以收到书了。如果你买的东西多,网站还提供免费的配送服务。

🔘 网上办公 Online working 🎧 06-03

A. 我是中国银行的分析师。我每天的工作都离不开互联网,我在网上收发电子邮件,得到最新的信息,然后分析这些信息。

B. 我是《经济日报》的记者。我们的报纸几年前就有了电子版,电子版的《经济日报》有报纸上的所有新闻和信息。人们在《经济日报》的网站上可以看到新闻,还可以很容易地找到几年前的信息。

C. 我是大学老师,过去学生想听我的课,都得来学校。现在有了互联网,我讲课的内容都可以上传到互联网上了,我的学生更多了。

D. 我是天马公司的经理。现在用网上办公软件发通知,节省了很多开会时间。有了企业微信以后,出差也可以用手机办公了。

网上办公 Online Working Lesson 6

口语任务 Speaking Tasks

1 网络会议 Online meeting 🎧 06-04

Xiāoshòu jīnglǐ: Guǎngzhōu de tóngshì, nǐmen hǎo! Nǐmen tīng de qīngchǔ ma?
销售 经理： 广州的同事，你们好！你们听得清楚吗？

Shēngchǎn jīnglǐ: Wǒmen tīng de hěn qīngchǔ. Niǔyuē de tóngshìmen hǎo!
生产 经理： 我们听得很清楚。纽约的同事们好！

Xiāoshòu jīnglǐ: Niǔyuē zhè biān de xiāoshòu hěn hǎo, nǐmen de shēngchǎn néng gēnshang ma?
销售 经理： 纽约这边的销售很好，你们的生产能跟上吗？

Shēngchǎn jīnglǐ: Xiànzài shì èrshísì xiǎoshí shēngchǎn, yídìng néng gēnshang.
生产 经理： 现在是24小时生产，一定能跟上。

Xiāoshòu jīnglǐ: Xīn huò shénme shíhou néng dào Niǔyuē?
销售 经理： 新货什么时候能到纽约？

Shēngchǎn jīnglǐ: Zhège xīngqīsì dào, bǎozhèng nǐmen zhōumò néng zhèngcháng xiāoshòu.
生产 经理： 这个星期四到，保证你们周末能正常销售。

Xiāoshòu jīnglǐ: Huò dào Niǔyuē yǐhòu, wǒ zài hé nǐmen liánxì.
销售 经理： 货到纽约以后，我再和你们联系。

Shēngchǎn jīnglǐ: Hǎode, wǒmen zài liánxì.
生产 经理：好的，我们再联系。

2 模拟练习 Simulation exercise

1 选词填空。Fill in the blanks with the proper words.

和　　到　　跟

① 这个星期四，新货能＿＿＿＿＿纽约。

② 我们是 24 小时生产，一定能＿＿＿＿＿上。

③ 货到以后，请＿＿＿＿＿我们联系。

2 根据以上对话，把两列句子搭配起来。Match the sentences on the right side with the ones on the left according to the dialogue above.

① 你们听得清楚吗？　　　　A. 现在是 24 小时生产，一定能跟上。

② 那边销售怎么样？　　　　B. 下周三。

③ 新货什么时候到？　　　　C. 我们听得很清楚。

④ 你们的生产能跟上吗？　　D. 情况很好。

网上办公
Online Working
Lesson 6

商务任务 Business Tasks

1　角色扮演 Role-play

- **角色 Roles**

  广州本田在广州、北京、上海的销售经理 Guangzhou Honda sales managers from Guangzhou, Beijing and Shanghai

- **任务 Assignment**

  在网上讨论本田汽车在广州、北京、上海的销售情况和下半年的营销计划。Discuss the sales of Honda in Guangzhou, Beijing and Shanghai, and the marketing project for the next half year.

2　商务体验 Business practice

浏览淘宝网（Taobao.com）网店，然后安排自己的网上商店的商品和服务，开一家淘宝店。Please visit Taobao's homepage, and then design your own E-store.

拓展 Exploration

1　超级链接 Super links

企业微信的应用

随着企业员工移动办公需求的日益增长，腾讯公司在 2016 年推出了企业微信。企业员工可以通过手机 APP 快速查找办公所需的企业资料，与同事进行沟通交流，完成打卡、办公流程审批，召开视频会议等。

- 通讯录：员工可以通过通讯录查询到所在企业所有同事的联系方式并通过企业微信与同事进行微信沟通。
- 视频会议：员工可以在手机上开会，还可以在线演示文档和共享屏幕。
- 群聊：管理者可以发起 2000 人以内的群聊，并在群内发布群公告、设置禁言。
- 打卡：员工可在手机上完成考勤打卡，管理者可以在手机上排班并发布。
- 汇报：员工可以随时随地用手机汇报工作进展，管理者可在手机端查阅员工报告。
- 审批：员工可以快速查看、上传办公文件，管理者可以通过手机进行审批。

2　商务小词库 Supplementary vocabulary

登录	dēnglù	log on
上传	shàngchuán	upload
下载	xiàzài	download
关键词	guānjiàncí	keyword
搜索引擎	sōusuǒ yǐnqíng	search engine
远程教育	yuǎnchéng jiàoyù	long-distance education
即时通信	jíshí tōngxìn	instant messaging
网络病毒	wǎngluò bìngdú	Internet virus

Lesson 7

Shìchǎng yíngxiāo
市场 营销
Marketing

学习目标 Objectives

1. 能用汉语简单描述消费行为　Be able to describe consumer behavior in Chinese
2. 能用汉语简单做市场分析　Be able to carry out a simple market analysis in Chinese
3. 能用汉语表达对广告的看法　Be able to express your opinion about advertising

词语 Words and Phrases　🎧 07-01

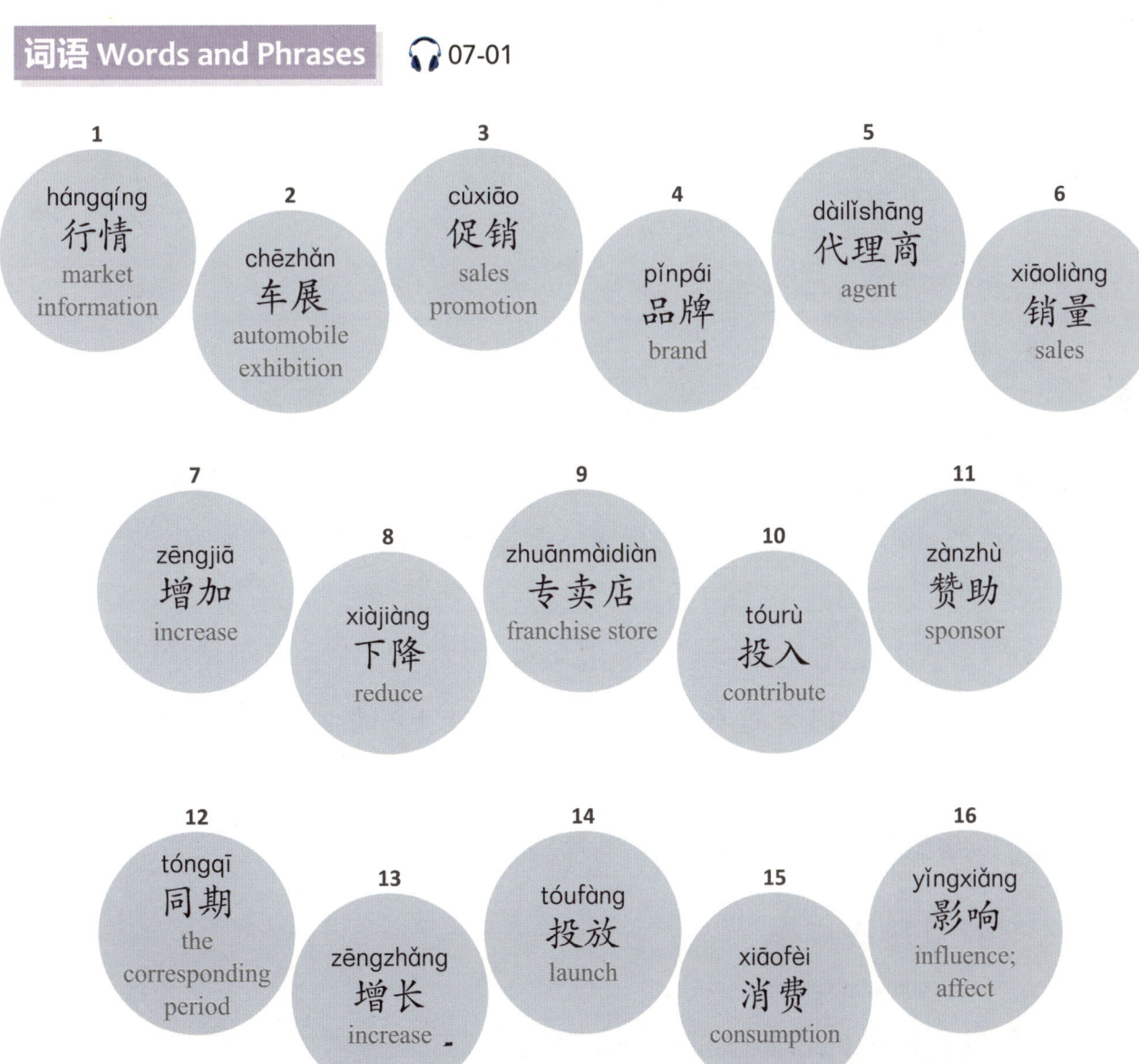

1. hángqíng 行情 market information
2. chēzhǎn 车展 automobile exhibition
3. cùxiāo 促销 sales promotion
4. pǐnpái 品牌 brand
5. dàilǐshāng 代理商 agent
6. xiāoliàng 销量 sales
7. zēngjiā 增加 increase
8. xiàjiàng 下降 reduce
9. zhuānmàidiàn 专卖店 franchise store
10. tóurù 投入 contribute
11. zànzhù 赞助 sponsor
12. tóngqī 同期 the corresponding period
13. zēngzhǎng 增长 increase
14. tóufàng 投放 launch
15. xiāofèi 消费 consumption
16. yǐngxiǎng 影响 influence; affect

49

关键句式 Key Sentence Patterns

1 购物 Shopping

……是买……的好时候。
It's a good time to buy...

例：现在是买车的好时候。

2 市场营销 Marketing

1）加大……投入

increase investment in...

例：我们开设了很多专卖店，加大了广告投入。

2）……比……同期增长……

From... to the same time in... increased by...

例：2015年这个品牌的手表销量比上一年同期增长了30%。

3 网络营销 Network marketing

投放网络广告

place online advertising

例：下一步我们计划投放网络广告。

市场营销
Marketing Lesson 7

听力任务 Listening Tasks

1　购买汽车 Buying a car　07-02

① 听一遍录音，然后在正确的信息后面画√。Listen to the recording, and then put a checkmark by the correct information.

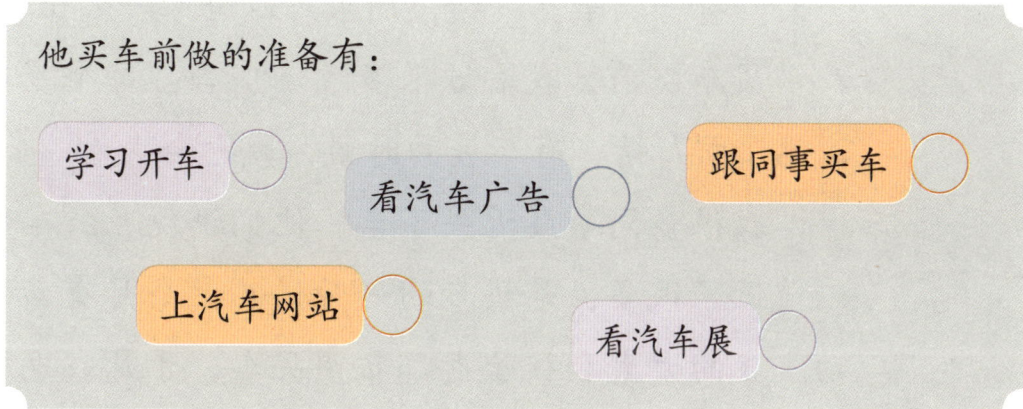

他买车前做的准备有：
学习开车　○
看汽车广告　○
跟同事买车　○
上汽车网站　○
看汽车展　○

② 再听一遍录音，然后用汉语复述这次买车经历。Listen to the record again, and then recount the experience of buying a car in Chinese.

2　产品销量 Product sales　07-03

① 听一遍录音，简单绘制两位代理商的产品销量走势。Listen to the recording, and then briefly draw up the two agents' product sale trends.

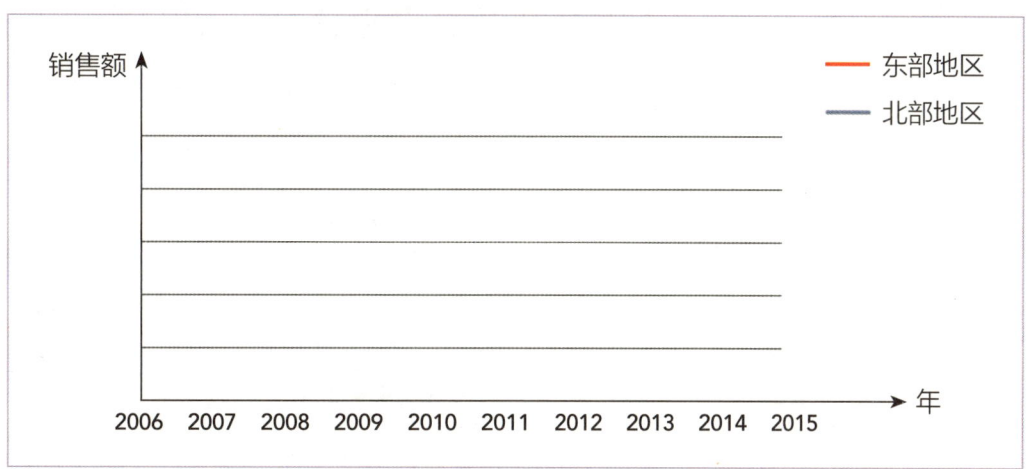

② 再听一遍录音，然后试着用汉语说说该品牌在两个地区的销量走势。Listen to the recording, and then try to introduce the sales trend of the brand in two regions in Chinese.

听力卡片 Listening Cards

🔘 购买汽车 Buying a car 🎧 07-02

我刚买了一辆汽车，星期六我们全家开车出去玩了一天。有一辆车真不错，周末可以全家一起出去玩。

买车以前，我看过很多汽车广告，每个星期在汽车网站了解行情，有车展的时候，我也会去看。

我很多同事最近买了车，他们说现在汽车的价格比以前低了很多，是买车的好时候。上个月有新的促销活动，我的太太和孩子也都希望买车，于是我也就买了一辆车，全家都很高兴。

🔘 产品销量 Product sales 🎧 07-03

代理商A：我是瑞士的一个品牌手表中国东部地区的代理商。我从2006年开始代理这个品牌。2010年的销量最高。从2011年开始，我们的广告投入虽然增加了，但销量一直没有增加，2012年销量开始下降。

代理商B：我也是这个品牌手表的中国代理商，我负责中国北部地区的销售。我从2010年开始代理这个品牌，2013年，我们开设了更多的专卖店，加大了广告投入，并开始赞助体育比赛。2015年的销量比上一年同期增长了80%。下一步我们计划投放网络广告。

市场营销
Marketing Lesson 7

口语任务 Speaking Tasks

1　广告的影响力 Advertising influence 🎧 07-04

Yíngxiāo rényuán: Nín měi tiān huì kàn shénme guǎnggào?
营销　人员：您每天会看什么广告？

Nǚ: Diànshì shang de guǎnggào hěn duō, wǒ kàn diànshì guǎnggào huì duō yìxiē.
女：电视上的广告很多，我看电视广告会多一些。

Yíngxiāo rényuán: Xiānsheng, nín měi tiān kàn shénme guǎnggào?
营销　人员：先生，您每天看什么广告？

Nán: Wǒ méi shíjiān kàn guǎnggào, búguò měi tiān kāichē de shíhou, huì tīng yìxiē diàntái de guǎnggào.
男：我没时间看广告，不过每天开车的时候，会听一些电台的广告。

Yíngxiāo rényuán: Xiǎopéngyou, nǐ xǐhuan kàn guǎnggào ma?
营销　人员：小朋友，你喜欢看广告吗？

Háizi: Tèbié xǐhuan. Wǒ zài guǎnggào li kànjiàn hǎochī de dōngxi jiù ràng māma gěi wǒ mǎi.
孩子：特别喜欢。我在广告里看见好吃的东西就让妈妈给我买。

Yíngxiāo rényuán: Tóngxué, guǎnggào duì nǐ de xiāofèi yǒu
营销　人员：同学，广告对你的消费有

> yǐngxiǎng ma?
> 影响 吗?
>
> Dàxuéshēng: Méiyǒu tài duō de yǐngxiǎng, wǒ gèng xǐhuan
> 大学生： 没有 太多 的 影响，我 更 喜欢
> zìjǐ liǎojiě chǎnpǐn de tèdiǎn.
> 自己 了解 产品 的 特点。

2 模拟练习 Simulation exercise

1 根据以上对话，把下面的人物与他们的回答连起来。Match the person with their opinions according to the dialogue above.

小朋友 •   • 听电台广告

女士 •   • 影响不大

大学生 •   • 买广告里好吃的东西

男士 •   • 看电视广告

2 根据实际情况，思考下面的问题，然后与你的同伴交流。Think about the following questions depending on the actual situation, and then exchange ideas with your partner.

① 你经常看广告吗?
② 广告对你的消费有什么影响?

市场营销 Marketing Lesson 7

商务任务 Business Tasks

1 角色扮演 Role-play

- **角色 Roles**
  联想公司在中国东部地区的代理商 Lenovo agent in East China

- **任务 Assignment**
  介绍联想电脑最近三年在中国东部地区的销售情况。Report the sales of Lenovo computers in the last three years.

2 商务体验 Business practice

请结合下列特点，向客户推销海尔冰箱。Promote Haier refrigerators to the customer according to the following specifications.

有名的品牌　　价格便宜

正在促销　　服务好

拓展 Exploration

1　超级链接 Super links

阿狸的网络营销

　　阿狸是中国当红原创动漫形象,其原型是一只可爱的小狐狸。迄今为止,阿狸的出版物销量已突破300万册,在线上拥有千万注册"粉丝"。阿狸品牌的成功离不开其出色的市场营销策略。阿狸的作者徐瀚说:"互联网给草根漫画家带来了机会,只需要将作品传到网上就可能被很多人关注。"他在2006年把阿狸的插画放上了各大网络论坛,又把阿狸制作成聊天表情包,阿狸从此在网上风靡。团队"乘胜追击",决定开发创作阿狸的衍生产品,并通过线上渠道进行销售。在淘宝、京东等各大电商平台,阿狸旗舰店应运而生。阿狸周边毛绒玩具、箱包、家居用品、服装配饰、书本文具……各种各样的生活小物,把阿狸从网络带进了现实,也进一步扩大了阿狸的市场和品牌影响力。

　　由于形象简单可爱,阿狸还深受许多其他品牌的青睐,麦考林服装、珂兰钻石等都是阿狸的合作商,会定期推出阿狸联名产品,与阿狸实现了互利共赢。

2　商务小词库 Supplementary vocabulary

定价	dìngjià	pricing
倾销	qīngxiāo	dumping
购买意向	gòumǎi yìxiàng	intention to buy
市场导向	shìchǎng dǎoxiàng	market-drive
零售	língshòu	retail
市场份额	shìchǎng fèn'é	market share
品牌形象	pǐnpái xíngxiàng	brand image
推出新产品	tuīchū xīn chǎnpǐn	launch a new product

Lesson 8

Cáiwù guǎnlǐ
财务管理
Financial Management

学习目标 Objectives

1. 了解公司的财务管理　Learn about the financial management of a company
2. 能分析汉语财务报表　Be able to analyze Chinese financial statements
3. 能做汉语财务计划　Be able to make a Chinese budget

词语 Words and Phrases  08-01

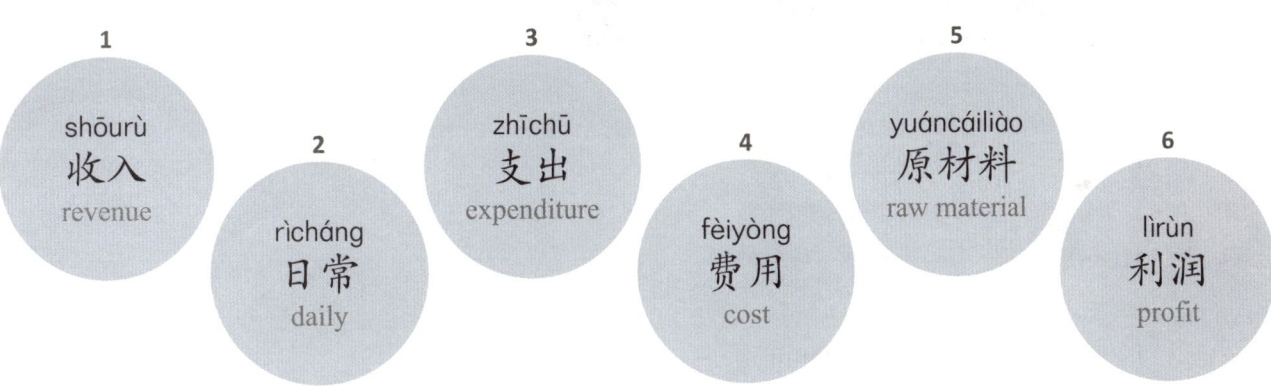

1. shōurù 收入 revenue
2. rìcháng 日常 daily
3. zhīchū 支出 expenditure
4. fèiyòng 费用 cost
5. yuáncáiliào 原材料 raw material
6. lìrùn 利润 profit

7. jiǎn 减 deduct
8. suǒdéshuì 所得税 income tax
9. jìng lìrùn 净利润 net profit
10. gōngzī 工资 salary
11. zūjīn 租金 rent

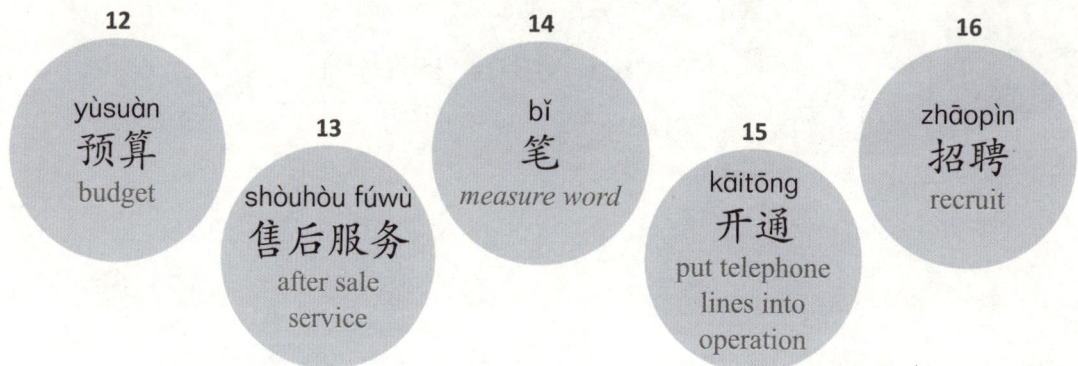

- 12 yùsuàn 预算 budget
- 13 shòuhòu fúwù 售后服务 after sale service
- 14 bǐ 笔 *measure word*
- 15 kāitōng 开通 put telephone lines into operation
- 16 zhāopìn 招聘 recruit

Měilì Fúzhuāng Diàn
美丽 服装 店
Meili Clothing Shop

关键句式 Key Sentence Patterns

1　财务计划 Financial planning

1) 增加/减少……费用
   increase/reduce the cost of...

   例：我们只能减少日常管理费用。

2) ……是什么用途?
   What is... for?

   例：增加的这笔钱是什么用途呢?

3) 和……谈谈
   have a talk with...

   例：我们得和财务经理好好谈谈。

财务管理 Financial Management   Lesson 8

听力任务 Listening Tasks

1 经营分析 Operational analysis 🎧 08-02

1 听一遍录音，然后完成天马公司的财务报表。Listen to the recording, and then complete the financial statements for the Tianma Company.

天马公司 2018 年财务报表	单位：万元
销售收入	
日常管理支出	
销售费用	
原材料支出	
利润	
净利润	

2 再听一遍录音，然后用汉语介绍天马公司 2018 年的经营情况。Listen to the recording again, and then introduce the operation of the Tianma Company in 2018 in Chinese.

2 收入和支出 Income and expenditures 🎧 08-03

1 听一遍录音，然后填空。Listen to the recording, and then fill in the blanks.

美丽服装店				单位：元
时间	销售收入	工资支出	商店租金	其他费用
9月			20000	10000
10月	90000		20000	
11月		35000	20000	

2 再听一遍录音，然后结合上表用汉语介绍美丽服装店 9—11 月的收支情况。Listen to the recording again, and then using the table above, describe the income and expenditures of the Meili Clothing Store from September to November in Chinese.

59

听力卡片 Listening Cards

🎧 **经营分析 Operational analysis** 08-02

因为生产的绿色食品销售得非常好，2018年天马公司的销售收入有8000万元。这一年，公司的日常管理支出是700万元，销售费用500万元，原材料支出500万元，天马公司得到6300万元的利润。在利润里要减去25%的所得税，天马公司2018年度的净利润大约是4725万元。

🎧 **收入和支出 Income and expenditures** 08-03

美丽服装店在过去3个月的收入和支出是这样的：9月销售收入8万元，工资支出2万元，商店租金2万元，其他费用1万元。10月销售收入9万元，工资支出2万8千元，商店租金2万元，其他费用8千元。11月销售收入10万元，工资支出3万5千元，商店租金2万元，其他费用9千元。

财务管理 Financial Management — Lesson 8

口语任务 Speaking Tasks

1 财务预算 Financial budget 🎧 08-04

董事长：明年的预算表你看了吗?

总经理：看过了。我觉得我们应该增加3%的售后服务费用。

董事长：增加的这笔钱是什么用途呢?

总经理：开通400免费客户服务电话，方便客户和我们联系。

董事长：明年要招聘新员工，人力资源的费用也得增加。

总经理：那我们只能减少日常管理费用了。

董事长：我们得和财务经理好好谈谈。

2　模拟练习 Simulation exercise

1 根据前页对话，把两列词语搭配起来。Match the words on the right side with the ones on the left according to the dialogue on the previous page.

减少　●　　　　　　　　　　●　新员工

开通　●　　　　　　　　　　●　客户和我们联系

招聘　●　　　　　　　　　　●　日常管理费用

方便　●　　　　　　　　　　●　客户服务电话

2 根据前页对话，填写下面的表格。Fill in the blanks according to the dialogue on the previous page.

财务预算表			
增加		费用，因为	
减少			

商务任务 Business Tasks

1　角色扮演 Role-play

- **角色** Roles

  A：售后服务经理　After-sales service manager

B：财务经理 Financial manager

• **任务** Assignment

售后服务经理跟财务经理讨论增加费用给客户提供更多售后服务的问题。Discuss the plan to increase the budget to offer more after sale service to the customers.

2　商务体验 Business practice

根据下表中欧力服饰公司 2016—2018 年的财务情况，为这家公司做出下一年的预算，并向财务经理汇报。Based on the financial situation from 2016 to 2018 shown in the table below, make a budget for Ouli Apparel Company for the coming year, and report it to the financial manager.

项目 时间	销售收入（万）	日常管理支出（万）	销售费用（万）	原材料（万）	利润（万）
2016 年	1000	50	80	500	370
2017 年	1100	80	140	600	280
2018 年	1500	130	200	850	320

拓展 Exploration

1　超级链接 Super links

华为的售后服务

作为中国最大的手机品牌之一，华为的成功离不开其贴心的售后服务。截至 2017 年底，华为已经在全球建成 1,400 多家线下服务中心，覆盖 105 个国家和地区；线上服务支持 65 种语言，已覆盖全球 111 个国家和地区。为了免去客户送修等待的烦恼，华为提供了远程维修服务。此外，华为还设立了"华为服务体验日"供用户体验华为的贴心服务。

成就客户是华为的企业核心价值观之一。华为坚信，为客户服务是华为存在的唯一理由，客户需求就是华为发展的原动力。因此，华为始终以客户为中心，快速响应客户需求，持续为客户创造长期价值。在成就客户的同时，华为也成就了自己。

2　商务小词库 Supplementary vocabulary

贷款	dàikuǎn	loan
信贷	xìndài	credit
资产	zīchǎn	assets
发票	fāpiào	invoice
增值税	zēngzhíshuì	value added tax
资产负债表	zīchǎn fùzhài biǎo	balance sheet
会计	kuàijì	accounting
账户	zhànghù	account

Lesson 9

Shāngyè zīxún
商业 咨询
Business Consulting

学习目标 Objectives

1. 能用汉语介绍商业咨询公司的基本情况
   Be able to introduce the basics of commercial consulting companies in Chinese
2. 能用汉语分析不同公司的经营特点
   Be able to analyze the management characteristics of different companies in Chinese
3. 能用汉语给企业提供咨询服务
   Be able to offer consultation services to companies in Chinese

词语 Words and Phrases  09-01

1. shāngyè 商业 business
2. zīxún 咨询 consulting
3. jiějué 解决 solve
4. fāng'àn 方案 plan
5. xìnxīn 信心 confidence
6. kuàguó gōngsī 跨国公司 multinational company
7. běntǔhuà 本土化 localization
8. fǎlǜ 法律 law
9. dānrèn 担任 serve as
10. gāojí 高级 senior
11. qǐyèjiā 企业家 entrepreneur
12. gùwèn 顾问 counselor

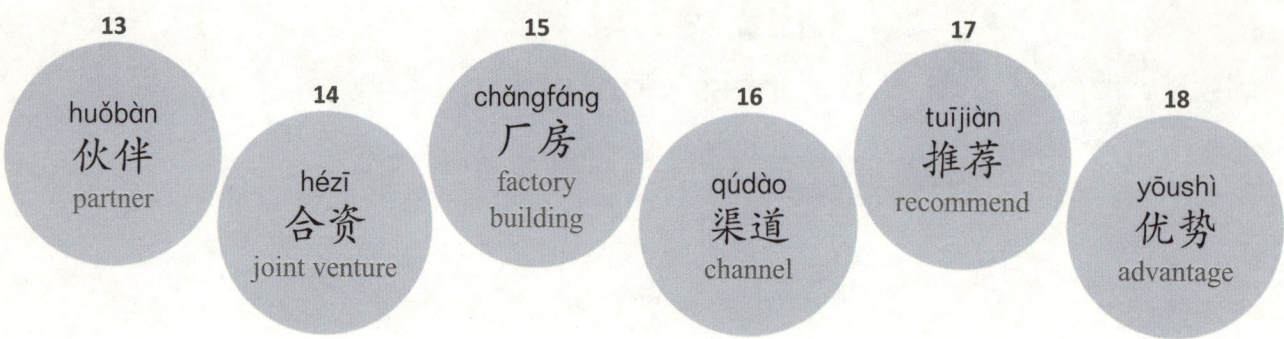

关键句式 Key Sentence Patterns

1 提供咨询服务 Offering consulting services

1) 向……提供……

supply... for...

例：我们向客户提供各种实用的解决方案。

2) 给……带来……

bring... to ...

例：我们有信心给客户带来利润。

3) 向……推荐

recommend... to ...

例：我向您推荐六家企业。

4) 有……优势

have an advantage in...

例：它们都有自己不同的经营或销售优势。

商业咨询 Business Consulting　Lesson 9

听力任务 Listening Tasks

1　咨询公司 The consulting company 🎧 09-02

1 听一遍录音，然后在关于这家公司的正确信息后画✓。Listen to the recording, and then put a checkmark by the correct information.

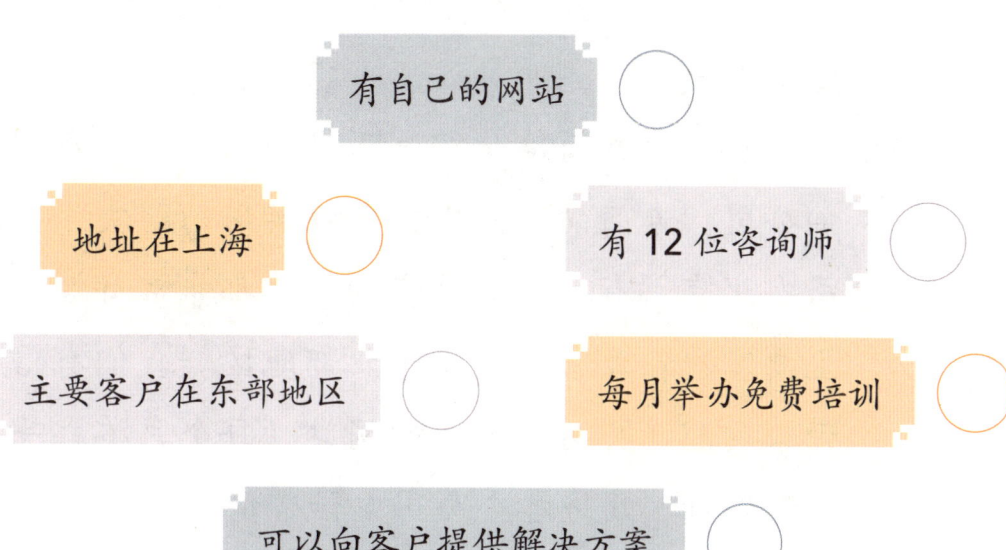

有自己的网站 ○

地址在上海 ○　　　有12位咨询师 ○

主要客户在东部地区 ○　　　每月举办免费培训 ○

可以向客户提供解决方案 ○

2 再听一遍录音，然后用汉语介绍这家公司。Listen to the recording again, and then introduce this company to the manager in Chinese.

2　跨国公司 The multinational companies 🎧 09-03

1 听一遍录音，然后把下面的国家或地区与他们的经营特点连起来。Listen to the recording, and then match the country with the management characteristic.

建立很多研发中心　生产本土化做得很好　中国人担任高级职位

67

2 再听一遍录音，然后用汉语介绍一家跨国公司。Listen to the recording again, and then introduce a multinational company.

听力卡片 Listening Cards

咨询公司 The consulting company 🎧 09-02

我给大家简单介绍一下我们的公司。我们是一家咨询公司，专门向客户提供各种实用的解决方案。我们公司在北京，有二十多位咨询师，都非常有经验。公司的主要客户在北京、天津等北部地区。我们有信心给客户带来利润。公司有自己的网站，每个月举办一次免费的管理培训，欢迎各个公司电话咨询。

跨国公司 The multinational companies 🎧 09-03

越来越多的跨国公司来到中国。不同跨国公司的本土化经营有不同的特点。比如说，日本公司的生产本土化做得很好，欧洲和美国公司在中国建立了很多研发中心。很多财务、法律和管理咨询公司也来到中国，为客户公司服务。另外，在欧美企业，中国人担任高级职位的也越来越多了。

Lesson 9 商业咨询 Business Consulting

口语任务 Speaking Tasks

1 商业咨询 Business consulting 🎧 09-04

企业家：Wǒmen yǐjīng zuòle hěn duō zhǔnbèi, xiànzài xīwàng néng jìnrù Guǎngzhōu shìchǎng.
我们已经做了很多准备，现在希望能进入广州市场。

顾问：Zhǎo yì jiā Guǎngzhōu de gōngsī zuò hézuò huǒbàn huì róngyì yìxiē.
找一家广州的公司做合作伙伴会容易一些。

企业家：Wǒmen kěyǐ tígōng hézī qǐyè de zījīn, jìshù hé guǎnlǐ fāng'àn.
我们可以提供合资企业的资金、技术和管理方案。

顾问：Nà jiù zhǎo kěyǐ tígōng chǎngfáng, yuángōng hé xiāoshòu qúdào de hézuò qǐyè.
那就找可以提供厂房、员工和销售渠道的合作企业。

企业家：Nǐ duì dāngdì de qǐyè yídìng hěn liǎojiě, nǐ néng gěi wǒ tuījiàn jǐ jiā ma?
你对当地的企业一定很了解，你能给我推荐几家吗？

顾问：Wǒ xiàng nín tuījiàn liù jiā qǐyè, tāmen dōu yǒu zìjǐ de jīngyíng huò xiāoshòu yōushì.
我向您推荐六家企业，他们都有自己的经营或销售优势。

Qǐyèjiā: Wǒ xiǎng xiān hé zuì yǒu xiāoshòu yōushì de jǐ jiā
企业家：我 想 先 和 最 有 销售 优势 的 几 家
qǐyè tántan.
企业 谈谈。

Gùwèn: Nà wǒ mǎshàng liánxì, ānpái nín hé tāmen jiànmiàn.
顾问：那我 马上 联系，安排您 和 他们 见面。

2 模拟练习 Simulation exercise

1 选词填空。Fill in the blanks with the proper words.

合作伙伴　　提供　　推荐

渠道　　优势

① 为了进入北京市场，公司想找一家可以提供销售_____的_____。

② 我们可以_____合资企业的资金、技术和管理。

③ _____几家在经营或销售方面有_____的企业。

2 根据以上对话，把两列词语搭配起来。Match the words on the right side with the ones on the left according to the dialogue above.

找　　　　　　　　　　资金

进入　　　　　　　　　见面

提供　　　　　　　　　合作伙伴

安排　　　　　　　　　北京市场

商业咨询
Business Consulting
Lesson 9

商务任务 Business Tasks

1 角色扮演 Role-play

- **角色** Roles
  - A：天马公司的市场部经理 Tianma Company marketing manager
  - B：一家咨询公司的咨询师 Consultant from a consulting company

- **任务** Assignment
  天马公司的有机食品现在希望进入上海市场，经理向咨询师咨询。Tianma organic food hopes to enter the Shanghai market. The manager consults with the consultant.

2 商务体验 Business practice

分析一下北京天天食品有限公司的经营情况，并给这家公司提出建议。Analyze the situation of the Beijng Tiantian Food Company, and then give some advice to this company.

2008年	天天食品有限公司在北京成立，以儿童食品为主。
2010年	成立营销部。
2013年	市场上出现了很多同类（tónglèi, similar）产品，这些企业都有自己有营销网络。
2013年	销售额开始逐年（zhú nián, year by year）下降。
2018年	产量增加，销售人员增加，销售额没有增加。

71

拓展 Exploration

1 超级链接 Super links

麦肯锡大中华分公司

麦肯锡大中华分公司包括北京、上海、深圳、香港和台北五个分公司。

近几年来，麦肯锡大中华分公司成功地在大中华地区开展了一系列项目，客户已遍及15个行业，还包括国家级、省市级及地区级的政府及机构，为国有企业、快速增长的高科技企业、领先的本地金融机构以及大中华区的跨国公司等各类客户提供了广泛的战略、组织和运营方面的咨询服务。

麦肯锡公司按照"全球一体"的模式运作，将麦肯锡全球专长及外部资源贡献给大中华区客户。

2 商务小词库 Supplementary vocabulary

报酬	bàochóu	payment
顾问委员会	gùwèn wěiyuánhuì	consultative committee
成长型企业	chéngzhǎngxíng qǐyè	start-up company
商业计划书	shāngyè jìhuà shū	business plan
创新	chuàngxīn	innovate
数据库	shùjùkù	data bank
对策	duìcè	countermeasure
外包	wàibāo	outsourcing

Lesson 10 战略管理
Zhànlüè guǎnlǐ
Strategy Management

学习目标 Objectives

1. 能用汉语描述公司战略的制订过程
   Be able to describe the strategic planning process in Chinese
2. 能用汉语介绍如何建立品牌　Be able to introduce how to establish a brand in Chinese
3. 能用汉语介绍改变战略的原因
   Be able to explain the reasons why a company changes its strategy in Chinese

词语 Words and Phrases 🎧 10-01

1. zhànlüè 战略 strategy
2. zhìdìng 制订 plan
3. guīmó 规模 scale
4. hángyè 行业 field
5. jìngzhēng duìshǒu 竞争对手 competitor
6. yùcè 预测 forecast
7. shìyìng 适应 adapt
8. yìngduì 应对 face up to
9. tiǎozhàn 挑战 challenge
10. xūqiú 需求 need
11. shòu huānyíng 受欢迎 be well received
12. shíshàng 时尚 fashionable
13. duōyuán 多元 diverse
14. zhīmíng 知名 famous
15. dàiyán 代言 represent

73

Haier 海尔

Hǎi'ěr
海尔
Haier

关键句式 Key Sentence Patterns

1　公司战略 Company strategy

1）满足……的需求
meet the needs of...

例：我们用最快的速度满足消费者的需求。

2）做出……品牌
create... brand

例：我们要求自己一定要做出本土化的品牌。

3）改变……战略
change the strategy of...

例：阿迪达斯好像已经改变了广告战略。

听力任务 Listening Tasks

1　制订公司战略 Develop a company strategy　🎧 10-02

1 听一遍录音，然后填空。Listen to the recording, and then fill in the blanks.

高飞做过的工作是：

☐ ➡ 公司　　☐ ➡ 高级 ☐

战略管理 Strategy Management   Lesson 10

2 再听一遍录音，然后根据录音将环节序号填入表内，完成流程图。Listen to the recording again, and then complete the flowchart by filling the correct numbers.

① 预测今后变化　　② 分析这些情况

③ 了解客户公司所在行业的情况

④ 了解客户公司竞争的情况

⑤ 了解客户公司规模、组织结构　　⑥ 制订战略

制订公司战略

□ → □ → □ → ⑥

3 再听一遍录音，然后用汉语介绍公司战略的制订过程。Listen to the recording again, and introduce the company strategy development process in Chinese.

2　建立品牌 Establishing the brand 🎧 10-03

1 听一遍录音，然后在海尔在欧美所采用的品牌战略后画✓。Listen to the recording, and then put a checkmark next to the brand strategies that Haier has adopted in Europe and America.

价格便宜 ○　　产品种类多 ○　　品牌本土化 ○

快速满足消费者的需求 ○　　售后服务好 ○

2 再听一遍录音，然后用下面的词语介绍一下海尔公司。Listen to the recording again, and then introduce the Haier Company using the following words.

听力卡片 Listening Cards

🔘 **制定公司战略 Developing a company strategy** 🎧 10-02

　　我叫高飞，是高级咨询师。我做咨询师六年了。以前我做过培训师，也做过公司总经理。作为高级咨询师，我的工作是帮助客户制订公司战略。在制订战略前，我和同事必须了解客户情况，比如公司规模、组织结构、客户所在行业、客户的竞争对手等。我和同事一起分析这些情况，预测今后的变化，为客户制订发展战略。比如客户应该怎么适应行业的变化，或者应对竞争对手的挑战等。

🔘 **建立品牌 Establishing the brand** 🎧 10-03

记者：海尔公司是一家知名的中国公司，那么公司的产品有哪些呢？

海尔员工：海尔的产品种类有很多，主要有冰箱、空调、洗衣机、电视机和厨房电器。

记者：为什么海尔公司会向美国和欧洲发展？

海尔员工：因为美国和欧洲市场要比其他国家大得多，那里有很多竞争对手，我们相信，如果能在欧美成功，那么在其他市场就更有可能成功。

记者：海尔是怎么在欧美市场建立品牌的呢？

海尔员工：第一，我们用最快的速度满足消费者的需求；第二，我们的产品种类很多，能满足不同人的需求；第三，我们要求自己一定要做出本土化的名牌。在美国，我们要让人们认为海尔是一个本土品牌，在欧洲，我们也希望做到这一点。

口语任务 Speaking Tasks

1 广告战略 Advertising strategy 10-04

Jìzhě: Zhè jǐ nián, Ādídásī yùndòngxié yuè lái yuè shòu huānyíng le.
记者：这几年，阿迪达斯运动鞋越来越受欢迎了。

Zhuānjiā: Yīnwèi chǎnpǐn de shèjì yuè lái yuè shíshàng le.
专家：因为产品的设计越来越时尚了。

Jìzhě: Wèi shénme ne?
记者：为什么呢？

专家： Yīnwèi shèjì hěn zhòngyào, yì shuāng bú piàoliang
专家：因为 设计 很 重要，一 双 不 漂亮
de yùndòngxié shì méi rén mǎi de.
的 运动鞋 是 没人 买 的。

记者： Gōngsī zěnme liǎojiě gè guó xiāofèizhě de xūqiú ne?
记者：公司 怎么 了解 各 国 消费者 的 需求 呢？

专家： Ādídásī shì yí ge duōyuán wénhuà de qǐyè,
专家：阿迪达斯 是 一个 多元 文化 的 企业，
yōngyǒu láizì yìbǎi duō ge guójiā de jìn liùqiān míng
拥有 来自 100 多 个 国家 的 近 6000 名
yuángōng, zài Dōngjīng hé Niǔyuē háiyǒu shèjìshì.
员工，在 东京 和 纽约 还有 设计室。

记者： Ādídásī hǎoxiàng yǐjīng gǎibiànle guǎnggào
记者：阿迪达斯 好像 已经 改变了 广告
zhànlüè.
战略。

专家： Gōngsī xiànzài qǐng shìjiè zhīmíng de yùndòngyuán、
专家：公司 现在 请 世界 知名 的 运动员、
yǎnyuán, gēshǒu wèi tāmen de pǐnpái dàiyán,
演员、歌手 为 他们 的 品牌 代言，
tóngshí yě zēngjiāle wǎngluò xiāoshòu.
同时 也 增加了 网络 销售。

2 模拟练习 Simulation exercise

根据以上对话，总结阿迪达斯公司的特点。Summarise the characteristics of Adidas according to the dialogue above.

- 产品设计：_____
- 了解消费者需求：_____
- 广告战略：_____

战略管理 Strategy Management Lesson 10

商务任务 Business Tasks

1 角色扮演 Role-play

- **角色** Roles

    A：方正集团的营销部经理 Founder Tech marketing manager
    B：咨询公司高级咨询师 Senior consultant from consulting agency

- **任务** Assignment

    方正集团为大学生设计了一款电脑。营销部经理向高级咨询师咨询新电脑的营销战略。The Founder Tech has designed a kind of computer for the college students. The marketing manager consults with a senior consultant.

2 商务体验 Business practice

华美公司是一家生产服装的企业，下面是这家公司的情况，请为华美公司制订发展战略。Huamei Company is a clothing company. The following is the company's current situation. Please plan a development strategy for Huamei Company.

	华美公司	竞争对手
优势	员工工作努力 产品质量好	品牌很知名 设计时尚
劣势	产品不知名 产品种类少	售后服务不太好 价格比较高
机会	市场需求很大	市场需求很大，很多公司想与它合作
挑战	刚刚进入这个行业，经验不足 行业竞争激烈	服装公司越来越多，产品种类越来越多

79

拓展 Exploration

1　超级链接 Super links

阿里巴巴商业生态圈

2016年9月,马云和他创办的阿里巴巴收购了肯德基(中国)的业务,一时成为新闻媒体关注的焦点。

马云是最早在中国开展电子商务并坚守在互联网领域的企业家之一,他创办的阿里巴巴集团在短时间内成为全球最大的网上贸易市场和商务交流社区之一。2014年9月19日,阿里巴巴集团在纽约证券交易所正式挂牌上市。2018年7月19日,《财富》世界500强排行榜全球同步发布,阿里巴巴集团排名第300位。

一直以来,阿里巴巴致力于形成更完整的商业生态圈。如今,阿里巴巴已成长为一个以电商为核心业务,涉及电商金融、本地生活服务、健康医疗、娱乐、智能终端等业务的完整商业生态圈。收购肯德基(中国),则可能是阿里巴巴在改变互联网、金融、物流行业之后,进军和改变餐饮业,尤其是快餐行业的重要信号。

2　商务小词库 Supplementary vocabulary

分包生产	fēnbāo shēngchǎn	subcontracting
垄断	lǒngduàn	monopoly
风险投资	fēngxiǎn tóuzī	venture capital
特许经营	tèxǔ jīngyíng	franchising
管理层收购	guǎnlǐcéng shōugòu	management buy-out (MBO)
投资人	tóuzīrén	investor
决策人	juécèrén	policy-maker
战术	zhànshù	tactic

Lesson 11

Qǐyè wénhuà 企业 文化
Enterprise Culture

学习目标 Objectives

1. 了解企业文化内涵　Learn about enterprise culture
2. 能用汉语表达企业文化　Be able to introduce the details of enterprise culture in Chinese
3. 能用汉语对比不同的企业　Be able to analyze different enterprise culture in Chinese

词语 Words and Phrases 🎧 11-01

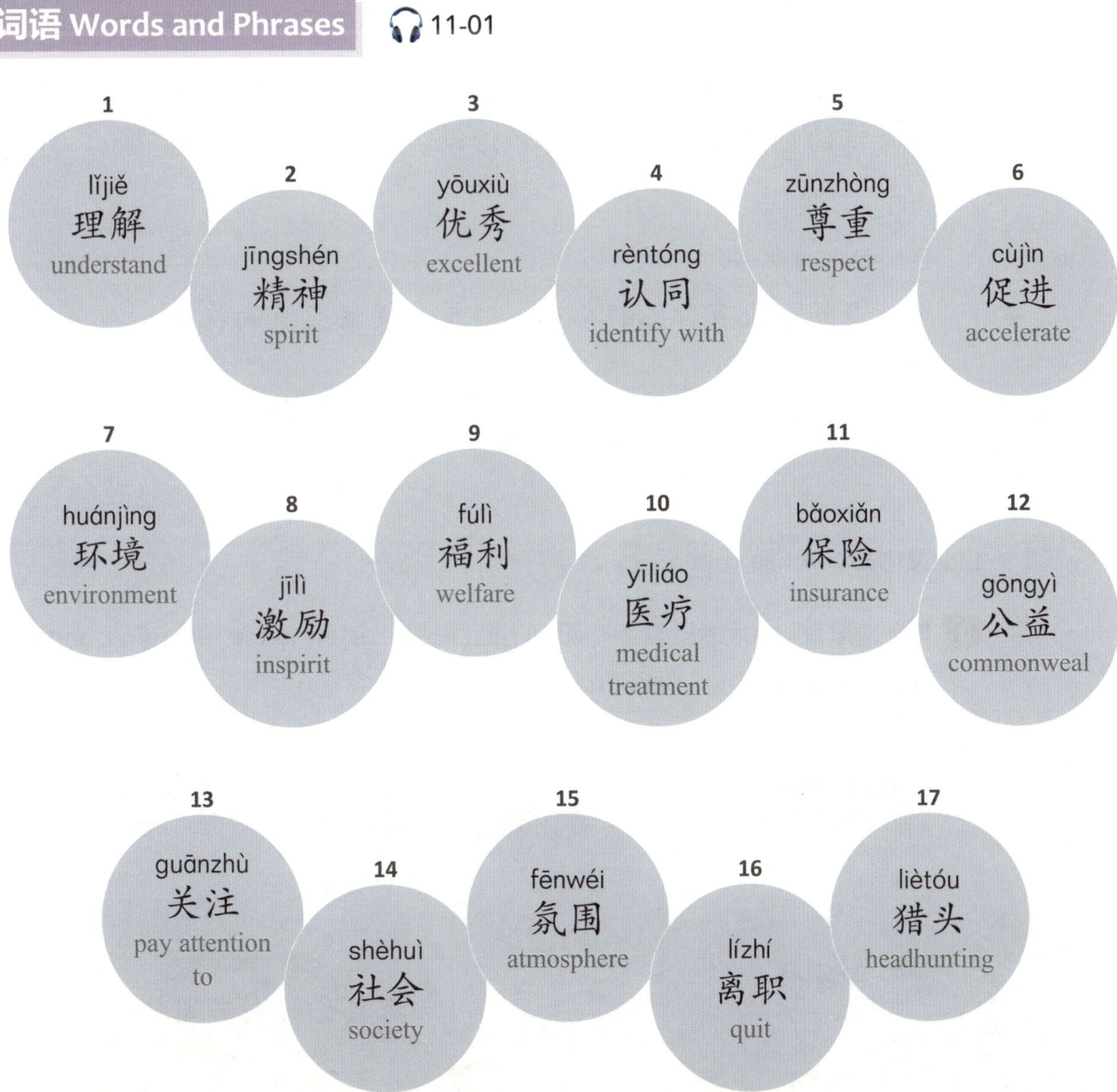

1. lǐjiě 理解 understand
2. jīngshén 精神 spirit
3. yōuxiù 优秀 excellent
4. rèntóng 认同 identify with
5. zūnzhòng 尊重 respect
6. cùjìn 促进 accelerate
7. huánjìng 环境 environment
8. jīlì 激励 inspirit
9. fúlì 福利 welfare
10. yīliáo 医疗 medical treatment
11. bǎoxiǎn 保险 insurance
12. gōngyì 公益 commonweal
13. guānzhù 关注 pay attention to
14. shèhuì 社会 society
15. fēnwéi 氛围 atmosphere
16. lízhí 离职 quit
17. liètóu 猎头 headhunting

Xīngbākè
星巴克
Starbucks

关键句式 Key Sentence Patterns

1 企业文化 Enterprise culture

1）为……组织……活动

organize... activity for...

例：有的企业为员工组织各种活动。

2）给……提供……机会

provide... opportunities for...

例：有的企业有自己的杂志，给员工提供交流的机会。

听力任务 Listening Tasks

1 企业文化 Enterprise culture 🎧 11-02

1 听一遍录音，然后圈出录音中提到的企业福利。Listen to the recording, and then circle the mentioned benefits.

医疗保险

去国外参加培训

组织各种活动

参加旅游

有自己的图书室

企业文化
Enterprise Culture   Lesson 11

2 再听一遍录音，然后用汉语说说你对企业文化的理解。Listen to the recording again, and then share your understanding of the enterprise culture.

2 喜欢星巴克 I like Starbucks 🎧 11-03

1 听一遍录音，然后圈出男的喜欢去星巴克的原因。Listen to the recording, and then circle the reasons why the man likes Starbucks.

价格便宜　　咖啡很好　　很方便　　环境好　　服务好　　企业文化优秀

2 再听一遍录音，然后用下面的词语介绍一下星巴克的企业文化。Listen to the recording again, and then introduce Starbucks' enterprise culture using the following words.

提供　　医疗保险　　关注　　参加　　公益活动　　社会责任

听力卡片 Listening Cards

💿 **企业文化** Enterprise culture 🎧 11-02

什么是企业文化呢？不同的企业家有不同的理解。有的企业家认为："企业文化就是企业的目标、企业的管理和企业的精神。"有的企业家认为："优秀的企业

83

文化应该让所有的员工都认同。因为员工对企业来说非常重要，企业和员工互相尊重可以促进共同发展。"还有的企业家认为："企业文化就是企业的环境，我们总是用企业的大环境影响每个员工。"

那么，怎么才能做好企业文化？有的企业为员工组织各种活动，给员工提供交流的机会；有的企业为了激励员工，每年会送优秀的员工去国外参加培训或旅游，作为员工的福利。

喜欢星巴克 I like Starbucks 🎧 11-03

男：我很喜欢星巴克的咖啡。

女：你为什么这么喜欢星巴克？因为咖啡还是因为别的？

男：当然是因为星巴克的咖啡好，还有是因为它就在办公楼的一层，很方便。

女：星巴克越开越多，为什么它会这么成功呢？

男：星巴克除了产品和服务很好，企业文化也很优秀。在美国，星巴克是第一个为所有员工提供完全医疗保险的公司。

女：听说星巴克公司还经常参加公益活动？

男：是的，星巴克在盈利的同时总是非常关注企业对社会的责任。

女：听了你的介绍，我现在也想喝它的咖啡了！

企业文化
Enterprise Culture
Lesson 11

口语任务 Speaking Tasks

1 不同的企业文化 Different enterprise cultures 🎧 11-04

Tián Lè: Nǐ de xīn gōngzuò zěnmeyàng?
田 乐：你的新 工作 怎么样？

Lǐ Yuè: Fēicháng hǎo, wǒ hěn mǎnyì.
李 月： 非常 好，我 很 满意。

Tián Lè: Gēn yǐqián bǐ yǒu shénme biànhuà?
田 乐：跟 以前 比 有 什么 变化？

Lǐ Yuè: Shōurù bǐ yǐqián dī yìxiē, dànshì fúlì hěn hǎo.
李 月： 收入 比 以前 低 一些，但是 福利 很 好。
Péixùn de jīhuì yě bǐ yǐqián duō le.
培训 的 机会 也 比 以前 多 了。

Tián Lè: Gōngzuò nèiróng hé huánjìng ne?
田 乐： 工作 内容 和 环境 呢？

Lǐ Yuè: Wǒ fùzé de gōngzuò gèng duō le, dànshì gōngzuò de
李 月：我 负责的 工作 更 多了，但是 工作 的
fēnwéi gèng qīngsōng yìxiē.
氛围 更 轻松 一些。

Tián Lè: Wǒ xiànzài de gōngzuò hěn méi yìsi, bùmén zhījiān
田 乐：我 现在 的 工作 很 没 意思，部门 之间
de hézuò yě bù hǎo, yìxiē tóngshì yǐjīng lízhí le.
的 合作 也 不好，一些 同事 已经 离职了。

Lǐ Yuè: Qǐyè bùtóng wénhuà yě bùtóng, rúguǒ nǐ bù néng
李 月：企业 不同 文化 也 不同，如果 你 不 能
jiēshòu xiànzài de qǐyè wénhuà, kěyǐ kǎolǜ huàn yí
接受 现在 的 企业 文化，可以 考虑 换 一
ge gōngzuò.
个 工作。

> Tián Lè: Yǐjīng yǒu lùetóu gōngsī hé wǒ liánxì le.
> 田 乐: 已经 有 猎头 公司 和 我 联系 了。
>
> Lǐ Yuè: Shōurù hé gōngzuò huánjìng dōu tèbié zhòngyào,
> 李 月: 收入 和 工作 环境 都 特别 重要,
> yídìng yào kǎolǜ hǎo
> 一定 要 考虑 好。

2 模拟练习 Simulation exercise

根据以上对话，写出李月的新工作有哪些变化。Write the changes that Li Yue's new job has undergone according to the dialogue above.

收　　入	
培训机会	
工作内容	
环　　境	

商务任务 Business Tasks

1 角色扮演 Role-play

- **角色** Roles

  A: 京东集团的赵文 Zhao Wen from JD.com
  B: 阿里巴巴集团的李平 Li Ping from Alibaba Group

- **任务** Assignment

  根据下面的情况谈谈各自公司的企业文化。Say something about the culture of two enterprise according to the information given below.

企业文化 Enterprise Culture — Lesson 11

赵文的公司
- 组织各种活动，员工交流机会多
- 培训机会多
- 部门之间合作很好
- 每年组织旅游

李平的公司
- 注重团队合作
- 非常关注对社会的责任
- 工作环境很好

2　商务体验 Business practice

根据这家公司几个员工的工作情况，分析公司的企业文化并向总经理提出你的建议。The following is the current situation of a company. Analyze their enterprise culture and give your suggestions.

前台
工作内容：每天接待客人，接电话。
工作安排：上午 8:00 — 下午 5:00（周一到周五）
　　　　　中午只能休息半个小时，吃饭时间很短。
个人感觉：不太喜欢目前的工作。因为很忙、很累，工资也很低。

财务部员工
工作内容：负责公司资金管理，做出生产预算等。
工作安排：上午 10:00 — 下午 8:00（周一到周六）
　　　　　因为工作太忙，经常工作到很晚。
个人感觉：很喜欢目前的工作，同事们合作得很好，工资还可以。但是办公室太小了，培训机会也不多。

市场部的员工
工作内容：负责市场的开发、广告设计、产品宣传等。
工作安排：上午 9:00 — 下午 6:00（周一到周五）
　　　　　经常出差，周末加班。
个人感觉：工作很有意思，但是工作环境不轻松。不喜欢周末工作，认为出差时应增加补助。

拓展 Exploration

1 超级链接 Super links

腾讯的企业文化

深圳市腾讯计算机系统有限公司成立于1988年，是中国最大的互联网综合服务提供商之一。2017年，腾讯在世界500强品牌榜单中位居第47名。

腾讯一直致力于做最受欢迎的互联网企业，不断倾听、满足用户需求，提升品牌形象，推动互联网行业共同发展，注重企业责任，赢得了来自用户、员工、行业和社会的共同尊重。腾讯希望能通过互联网提升人们的生活品质，通过提供个性化、人性化的服务，为人们带来便捷和愉悦。

腾讯内部有一套完整的人才培养体系，员工可以在不同的职业发展阶段选择适合自己的培训类别，结合特长和兴趣选择适合自己的发展通道。腾讯努力为员工提供更好、更有利的学习环境和氛围，这也是腾讯吸引并留住员工的一大有利因素。

腾讯拥有专门的公益平台——腾讯公益，历史善款总额高达46亿元人民币，腾讯公司还曾在2011年、2012年连续两年荣获"中华慈善奖"，为公益事业做出了巨大贡献。

2 商务小词库 Supplementary vocabulary

风险	fēngxiǎn	risk
使命	shǐmìng	mission
价值观	jiàzhíguān	value
文化差异	wénhuà chāyì	cultural difference
奖金	jiǎngjīn	bonus
忠诚	zhōngchéng	loyal
开放	kāifàng	open
自律	zìlǜ	self discipline

Lesson 12 社会 贡献
Shèhuì gòngxiàn
Social Contribution

学习目标 Objectives

1. 能用汉语介绍企业的社会贡献
   Be able to introduce the social contributions of enterprises in Chinese
2. 能用汉语介绍一些慈善活动　Be able to introduce charity activities in Chinese
3. 能用汉语说明如何举办慈善活动
   Be able to introduce how to prepare charity activities in Chinese

词语 Words and Phrases　🎧 12-01

1. gòngxiàn 贡献 contribution
2. císhàn 慈善 charity
3. pāimài 拍卖 auction
4. zhǔchí 主持 host
5. míngxīng 明星 celebrity
6. kǎochá 考察 investigate
7. tóuzī 投资 invest
8. chóují 筹集 raise
9. shànkuǎn 善款 donation
10. zérèn gǎn 责任感 sense of responsibility
11. zǒngcái 总裁 CEO
12. jiàzhí 价值 value
13. pínkùn 贫困 poor
14. xuéyè 学业 study
15. gōngyìpǐn 工艺品 craftwork
16. jīngměi 精美 exquisite
17. yāoqǐnghán 邀请函 invitation
18. quèrèn 确认 affirm

89

Gāojí Gōngshāng Guǎnlǐ Shuòshì
高级 工商 管理 硕士（EMBA）
Executive Master of Business Administration

Nèiménggǔ
内蒙古
Inner Mongolia

关键句式 Key Sentence Patterns

1 慈善拍卖 Charity auction

可以帮助……
can help...

例：拍卖收入可以帮助中国西部地区的孩子完成中学的学习。

2 慈善精神 Charitable spirit

增强……的社会责任感
increase ...'s sense of social responsibility

例：这次活动为了是增强学生的社会责任感。

听力任务 Listening Tasks

1 慈善拍卖晚会 Charity auction gala 🎧 12-02

听一遍录音，然后填空。Listen to the recording, and then fill in the blanks.

时　　间：_____
地　　点：_____
拍卖物品：_____、工艺品、_____
主 持 人：_____、电影明星

社会贡献
SOCIAL CONTRIBUTION
Lesson 12

2 再听一遍录音，然后完成邀请函，并用汉语邀请你的同伴参加本次晚会。Listen to the recording again, then finish the invitation and invite your partner to attend the gala in Chinese.

慈善晚会邀请函

_____先生／女士：

您好！

为了帮助贫困地区的儿童_____，我公司定于11月26日（星期_____）晚_____点至10点，在_____一层宴会厅举行2020年"平安之夜"慈善拍卖晚会。

我们真诚地邀请您参加！如果您想了解更多的情况，请随时与我们联系。我们希望在11月15日前得到您能否出席的确切消息。

此致

敬礼

平安基金会

张明（总经理）

2020年10月31日

2 公益活动 Public activities 🎧 12-03

1 听一遍录音，然后选择正确答案。Listen to the recording, and then choose the correct answer.

EMBA学员去内蒙古的目的是：_____

① 了解当地经济发展和投资环境　② 培训中学老师

③ 举办文化活动　④ 增强社会责任感

2 再听一遍录音，然后用汉语介绍这次活动。Listen to the recording again, and then introduce this activity in Chinese.

听力卡片 Listening Cards

慈善拍卖晚会 Charity auction gala 12-02

男：我想邀请你和我一起参加慈善拍卖晚会。

女：好啊。什么时间？在哪儿？

男：下星期四晚上8点，在北京饭店。

女：有什么活动呢？

男：先是晚宴，然后是拍卖。

女：这次拍卖一些什么东西呢？

男：有名牌服装、工艺品和手表等。

女：谁主持这次拍卖？

男：晚会请了知名的拍卖师和一位电影明星一起主持拍卖。

女：拍卖的收入做什么用呢？

男：帮助中国贫困地区的儿童完成学业。

女：那我一定得买一些东西。

公益活动 Public activities 12-03

近年来，越来越多的企业管理者开始重视企业的社会贡献。今年，某大学EMBA的18名学员来到内蒙古，考察当地的经济发展和投资环境。他们在内蒙古举办了多种公益活动，筹集善款100万元，用于培训当地的中学老师。这所大学的老师表示，EMBA课程更应该注重学员社会责任感的培养。海尔集团总裁也曾说，"一个企业如果没有为社会贡献价值，这样的企业就不应该存在"。

社会贡献 SOCIAL CONTRIBUTION Lesson 12

口语任务 Speaking Tasks

1 慈善拍卖筹备 Preparing the charity auction 🎧 12-04

Dǒngshìzhǎng: Gōngsī xià ge yuè jǔbàn de císhàn pāimài wǎnhuì, nǐ zhǔnbèi de zěnmeyàng le?
董事长：公司下个月举办的慈善拍卖晚会，你准备得怎么样了？

Jīnglǐ: Zhōngguó shūfǎ, huìhuà zuòpǐn hái yǒu gōngyìpǐn dōu zhǔnbèi hǎo le.
经理：中国书法、绘画作品还有工艺品都准备好了。

Dǒngshìzhǎng: Wǒ xiǎng tāmen yídìng fēicháng jīngměi.
董事长：我想它们一定非常精美。

Jīnglǐ: Shìde, pāimài de shōurù kěyǐ bāngzhù yìbǎi ge pínkùn dàxuéshēng wánchéng xuéyè.
经理：是的，拍卖的收入可以帮助100个贫困大学生完成学业。

Dǒngshìzhǎng: Běijīng Fàndiàn de yànhuìtīng liánxì hǎo le ma?
董事长：北京饭店的宴会厅联系好了吗？

Jīnglǐ: Liánxì hǎo le, wǒmen hái qǐngle zhīmíng pāimàishī Fāng xiānsheng wèi wǒmen zhǔchí pāimài.
经理：联系好了，我们还请了知名拍卖师方先生为我们主持拍卖。

Dǒngshìzhǎng: Yào gěi suǒyǒu de gōngsī kèhù fā yāoqǐnghán, hái yào dǎ diànhuà quèrèn.
董事长：要给所有的公司客户发邀请函，还要打电话确认。

> Jīnglǐ: Dàjiā duì zhège císhàn pāimài huódòng dōu hěn gǎn xìngqù, bǎifēnzhī bāshí de kèhù quèrèn tāmen huì cānjiā wǎnhuì.
> 经理：大家 对 这个 慈善 拍卖 活动 都 很 感 兴趣，80% 的客户 确认 他们 会 参加 晚会。

2 模拟练习 Simulation exercise

1 根据以上对话，把两列词语搭配起来。Match the words on the right side with the ones on the left according to the dialogue above.

举办　　　　　　　　　　慈善拍卖会

知名的　　　　　　　　　拍卖师

打电话　　　　　　　　　邀请函

发　　　　　　　　　　　确认

主持　　　　　　　　　　拍卖

2 根据以上对话，回答下列问题。Answer the questions according to the dialogue above.

① 这家公司为什么要举办拍卖晚会？

② 谁主持这家公司的拍卖会？

③ 拍卖的内容有哪些？

社会贡献 Social Contribution Lesson 12

商务任务 Business Tasks

1 角色扮演 Role-play

- **角色 Roles**
  A：公司公关经理 Public relations manager
  B：公司客户 Client

- **任务 Assignment**
  为了帮助中国西部地区的孩子完成学业，公关经理打电话邀请公司客户参加慈善拍卖晚会。To help the children from the west of China finish school, The public relations manager invites the clients to attend the charity auction gala by phone.

2 商务体验 Business practice

了解一次慈善捐款（物）活动，介绍它的目的、组织者以及所捐款（物）情况。Get to know some charity programs, and introduce their objectives, organizers, and donation status.

拓展 Exploration

1 超级链接 Super links

万达集团的企业使命

中国万达集团以"共创财富,公益社会"为使命。万达董事长曾说:"万达的发展,不光是为自己,更是为社会做贡献,奋斗创造的财富最终要还给社会。"

在社会公益方面,自1988年创立以来,万达集团奉献给社会慈善事业的资金累计超过58亿元,项目涉及幼儿园、小学、中学等学校建设,汶川、玉树等抗震救灾捐助,中国足球振兴,文化遗址修复等多个领域,多次获得国家"中华慈善奖""消除贫困奖"等奖项。

在创造就业方面,万达集团连续多年成为全国创造就业领先的企业。为了鼓励大学生创业,万达集团还推出了"支持大学生创业十年计划",并成立了创业指导部,给予大学生创业专业指导。

此外,万达集团也是全国最早推行节能建筑的企业。

2 商务小词库 Supplementary vocabulary

道德	dàodé	ethics
捐赠	juānzèng	donate
感激	gǎnjī	appreciate
社区	shèqū	community
公民	gōngmín	citizen
义务	yìwù	obligation
共同利益	gòngtóng lìyì	common interests

词语表 Vocabulary Index

第1课

初次	chū cì	first time
记者	jìzhě	journalist
店长	diànzhǎng	store manager
工程师	gōngchéngshī	engineer
交流	jiāoliú	exchange
经验	jīngyàn	experience
发言	fāyán	make a statement
主管	zhǔguǎn	person in charge
经理	jīnglǐ	manager
培训师	péixùnshī	trainer
分析师	fēnxīshī	analyst
广告	guǎnggào	advertisement
部	bù	department
人力资源	rénlì zīyuán	human resources

专有名词

经济日报	Jīngjì Rìbào	Economic Daily
麦当劳	Màidāngláo	McDonald's
华为	Huáwéi	Huawei
广州本田	Guǎngzhōu Běntián	Guangzhou Honda
支付宝	Zhīfùbǎo	Alipay
京东网	Jīngdōng Wǎng	JD.com
阿迪达斯	Ādídásī	Adidas
中国银行	Zhōngguó Yínháng	Bank of China

第2课

团队	tuánduì	team
员工	yuángōng	staff
部门	bùmén	department
研发	yánfā	research and development
市场	shìchǎng	market
产品	chǎnpǐn	product
营销	yíngxiāo	marketing
财务	cáiwù	finance
运营	yùnyíng	arrange
生产	shēngchǎn	produce
经营	jīngyíng	manage
管理	guǎnlǐ	administration
负责	fùzé	in charge of
开发	kāifā	develop
销售	xiāoshòu	sell
秘书	mìshū	secretary
申请	shēnqǐng	apply
职位	zhíwèi	position
录用	lùyòng	hire

专有名词

天马公司	Tiānmǎ Gōngsī	Tianma Company
北京大学	Běijīng Dàxué	Peking University

第3课

日程	rìchéng	schedule
安排	ānpái	arrangement
预订	yùdìng	book; reserve
往返票	wǎngfǎn piào	round-trip ticket
经济舱	jīngjì cāng	economy class
公务舱	gōngwù cāng	business class
企业	qǐyè	enterprise
总结	zǒngjié	summary
工厂	gōngchǎng	factory
查看	chákàn	check
沟通	gōutōng	communicate
车间	chējiān	workshop (in factory)
客户	kèhù	customer

专有名词

中国国际航空公司（国航）	Zhōngguó Guójì Hángkōng Gōngsī (Guó Háng)	Air China
东京	Dōngjīng	Tokyo

第4课

办公	bàngōng	handle official business
地点	dìdiǎn	location

集团	jítuán	group
电梯	diàntī	elevator; lift
指示图	zhǐshì tú	indicater diagram
清洁	qīngjié	clean
责任	zérèn	responsibility
值班	zhíbān	on duty
前台	qiántái	receptionist
快递员	kuàidìyuán	deliveryman
订购	dìnggòu	order
家具	jiājù	furniture
配送	pèisòng	deliver
牌子	páizi	sign

专有名词

| 顺丰速运 | Shùnfēng Sùyùn | SF Express |

第5课

宴会	yànhuì	banquet
酒店	jiǔdiàn	hotel
随意	suíyì	feel free to
举办	jǔbàn	hold
画廊	huàláng	gallery
合作	hézuò	coorporation
愉快	yúkuài	pleasant
同事	tóngshì	colleague
庆祝	qìngzhù	celebrate
合作商	hézuòshāng	official partner
质量	zhìliàng	quality
合理	hélǐ	reasonable
进口	jìnkǒu	import
成功	chénggōng	successful
干杯	gānbēi	cheers

专有名词

北海公园	Běihǎi Gōngyuán	Beihai Park
北京饭店	Běijīng Fàndiàn	Beijing Hotel
王府井	Wángfǔjǐng	Wangfujing
全聚德烤鸭店	Quánjùdé Kǎoyā Diàn	Quanjude Roast Duck Restaurant

第6课

折扣	zhékòu	discount
过程	guòchéng	process
网站	wǎngzhàn	website

地址	dìzhǐ	address
付款	fùkuǎn	pay
提交	tíjiāo	submit
信息单	xìnxī dān	information sheet
提供	tígōng	provide
免费	miǎnfèi	free
电子版	diànzǐ bǎn	electronic edition
上传	shàngchuán	upload
互联网	hùliánwǎng	Internet
软件	ruǎnjiàn	software
通知	tōngzhī	notice
联系	liánxì	contact

专有名词

| 企业微信 | Qǐyè Wēixìn | WeChat Work |
| 纽约 | Niǔyuē | New York City |

第7课

行情	hángqíng	market information
车展	chēzhǎn	automobile exhibition
促销	cùxiāo	sales promotion
品牌	pǐnpái	brand
代理商	dàilǐshāng	agent
销量	xiāoliàng	sales
增加	zēngjiā	increase
下降	xiàjiàng	reduce
专卖店	zhuānmàidiàn	franchise store
投入	tóurù	contribute
赞助	zànzhù	sponsor
同期	tóngqī	the corresponding period
增长	zēngzhǎng	increase
投放	tóufàng	launch
消费	xiāofèi	consumption
影响	yǐngxiǎng	influence; affect

专有名词

| 瑞士 | Ruìshì | Switzerland |

第8课

收入	shōurù	revenue
日常	rìcháng	daily
支出	zhīchū	expenditure

词语表
Vocabulary Index

费用	fèiyòng	cost
原材料	yuáncáiliào	raw material
利润	lìrùn	profit
减	jiǎn	deduct
所得税	suǒdéshuì	income tax
净利润	jìng lìrùn	net profit
工资	gōngzī	salary
租金	zūjīn	rent
预算	yùsuàn	budget
售后服务	shòuhòu fúwù	after sale service
笔	bǐ	*measure word*
开通	kāitōng	put telephone lines into operation
招聘	zhāopìn	recruit

专有名词

美丽服装店	Měilì Fúzhuāng Diàn	Meili Clothing Shop

第 9 课

商业	shāngyè	business
咨询	zīxún	consulting
解决	jiějué	solve
方案	fāng'àn	plan
信心	xìnxīn	confidence
跨国公司	kuàguó gōngsī	multinational company
本土化	běntǔhuà	localization
法律	fǎlǜ	law
担任	dānrèn	serve as
高级	gāojí	senior
企业家	qǐyèjiā	entrepreneur
顾问	gùwèn	counselor
伙伴	huǒbàn	partner
合资	hézī	joint venture
厂房	chǎngfáng	factory building
渠道	qúdào	channel
推荐	tuījiàn	recommend
优势	yōushì	advantage

专有名词

日本	Rìběn	Japan
欧洲	Ōuzhōu	Europe
美国	Měiguó	the United States

第 10 课

战略	zhànlüè	strategy
制订	zhìdìng	plan
规模	guīmó	scale
行业	hángyè	field
竞争对手	jìngzhēng duìshǒu	competitor
预测	yùcè	forecast
适应	shìyìng	adapt
应对	yìngduì	face up to
挑战	tiǎozhàn	challenge
需求	xūqiú	need
受欢迎	shòu huānyíng	be well received
时尚	shíshàng	fashionable
多元	duōyuán	diverse
知名	zhīmíng	famous
代言	dàiyán	represent

专有名词

海尔	Hǎi'ěr	Haier

第 11 课

理解	lǐjiě	understand
精神	jīngshén	spirit
优秀	yōuxiù	excellent
认同	rèntóng	identify with
尊重	zūnzhòng	respect
促进	cùjìn	accelerate
环境	huánjìng	environment
激励	jīlì	inspirit
福利	fúlì	welfare
医疗	yīliáo	medical treatment
保险	bǎoxiǎn	insurance
公益	gōngyì	commonweal
关注	guānzhù	pay attention to
社会	shèhuì	society
氛围	fēnwéi	atmosphere
离职	lízhí	quit
猎头	liètóu	headhunting

专有名词

星巴克	Xīngbākè	Starbucks

第12课

贡献	gòngxiàn	contribution
慈善	císhàn	charity
拍卖	pāimài	auction
主持	zhǔchí	host
明星	míngxīng	celebrity
考察	kǎochá	investigate
投资	tóuzī	invest
筹集	chóují	raise
善款	shànkuǎn	donation
责任感	zérèn gǎn	sense of responsibility
总裁	zǒngcái	CEO
价值	jiàzhí	value
贫困	pínkùn	poor
学业	xuéyè	study
工艺品	gōngyìpǐn	craftwork
精美	jīngměi	exquisite
邀请函	yāoqǐnghán	invitation
确认	quèrèn	affirm

专有名词

高级工商管理硕士（EMBA）	Gāojí Gōngshāng Guǎnlǐ Shuòshì	Executive Master of Business Administration
内蒙古	Nèiménggǔ	Inner Mongolia

翻译 Translation

第 1 课

口语任务·介绍自己

A: Hello! Are you the new person?
B: Yes, today is my first day of work here.
A: Welcome! My name is Liu Ping, I work in the advertising department.
B: Nice to meet you. My name is Li Hong. I work in the human resource department.
A: If you need any help, please let me know.
B: Thank you very much.

拓展·超级链接·交换名片

Exchanging Business Cards

When people exchange business cards on the first meeting, you'd better use both hands or right hand to give the card to others. Generally speaking, it is necessary to say some polite words, such as *Qing duo zhijiao* (I would appreciate your valuabe guidance)", "*Duo lianxi* (contact me more)", "*Qing huicun* (please keep the card)" and so on. In addition, when you meet with several people, you should first give your card to the person with the highest position.

If you receive someone's business card, you must receive it with both hands to show your politenees, and you should also express gratitude. For example, if someone says to you "*Duo zhijiao* (I would appreciate your valuable guidance)", you should say "*Bu keqi* (you're welcome)" or "*Bici bici* (same to you)".

While there are many titles on a name card, in general, the first title is the most important.

When you introduce someone to others, you should introduce the person with the highest position to the person with the lower position. If you are talking to someone, it is best to refer to them by their official title, such as "Wang Zong (Manager Wang)" or "Li Dong (President Li)."

第 2 课

口语任务·面试

Interviewer: Please briefly introduce yourself.
Interviewee: I graduated from Peking University in 2010. I have worked in a computer company for three years.
Interviewer: Why did you apply for the position of marketing manager?
Interviewee: Because I have five years' experience in marketing.
Interviewer: When can you start work, if we hire you?
Interviewee: I can start work as soon as possible.

拓展·超级链接·小米科技的管理模式

Xiaomi Tech's Management Model

Xiaomi Tech promotes an innovative and high-speed Internet culture, in which all employees can maximize their creativity in a relaxed and cooperative work environment. When talking about the Xiaomi team, it is necessary to mention Xiaomi's "flat organization" management model—each department, from production to marketing, from hardware to e-commerce, is closely monitored by one of the founders, who personally guides employees. The departments do not interfere with each other, but rather, work together to perform each of their own tasks more effectively. This kind of management system can ensure the speed of information transmission, enable the higher-level to quickly discover the actual problems reflected by the information, and make timely decisions; and at the same time, greatly improve the team's organizational response and coordination capabilities, spark employees' active initiative and innovative spirit, and through all of this, increase the team's work efficiency.

第 3 课

口语任务 · 日常工作

Journalist: Could you please say something about your daily work?
Akira Mishima: I often come to the factory at 8:00 am. First I check my e-mail, and then find out about yesterday's production.
Journalist: How do you communicate with other managers?
Akira Mishima: We have a regular meeting every morning.
Journalist: What about the afternoon?
Akira Mishima: I often stay at the workshop.
Journalist: When do you leave?
Akira Mishima: Around 6:00 pm. But I have to meet customers sometimes.

拓展 · 超级链接 · 注重个人和团队的共同力量

Value the Shared Power of the Individual and the Team

The Gree Company expects employees not only demonstrate good characters, but also to be able to become united as a group, help one another, and advance together.

The Gree Company encourages employees to actively participate in team meetings, and voice their thoughts at team meetings. The company gives awards and honors to employees who eagerly speak. The company also often organizes group activities to foster team spirit among the employees.

The power of the team is limitless. Through these activities, the Gree Company wants to help employees establish community awareness, give full play to their strengths, and make valuable contributions to the team.

第 4 课

口语任务 · 公司地址

Receptionist: Hello! This is Tianma Company.
deliveryman: Hello! This is SF Express. You have ordered some office furniture which we will deliver for you right now. Could you please tell us the easiest way to find you?
Receptionist: First you go to the southwest gate of Peking University. You will see a Bank of China next to the gate. Our company sign is across the street at the entrance.
deliveryman: OK. Your company is opposite the Bank of China which is next to the southwest gate of Peking University.
Receptionist: Yes, that's right. If you have any problems, please call us again.
deliveryman: Thank you. Bye.

拓展 · 超级链接 · 快递在中国

Express Delivery in China

With the development of electronic commerce, China's express delivery industry has become more and more advanced. Anything from a pair of socks to a refrigerator can be shipped via express delivery. Now that there's express delivery, you can eat grapes from Xinjiang or Chinese mitten crabs from Jiangsu even if you're in Beijing. On rainy days and sunny days alike, you can see deliverymen out and about on the streets. This development has also provided more employment opportunities for Chinese people. At the same time, express delivery has given rise to the development of other industries, such as online pharmacies, online florists, online restaurants, and beyond. In summary, express delivery has made Chinese people's lives more convenient.

第 5 课

口语任务 · 商务宴会

Sales Manager: It's our pleasure to corporate with you. To celebrate our successful corporation, I want to invite you and your colleagues to a dinner.
Official Partner: Thank you. It is also our pleasure.
Sales Manager: I'll wait for you at 7:00 pm tomorrow evening at the entrance of Wangfujing Quanjude Roast Duck Restaurant. Is that OK?
Official Partner: That's great. We all like roast duck.

See you tomorrow at 7:00.

(At the banquet)

Official Partner: Your coats are of good quality and reasonable prices, so we will import another 10000 coats next time.

Sales Manager: This kind of the coat sells good in China. Here's to our successful corporation. Cheers!

Official Partner: And to our future corporation. Cheers!

⊃ 拓展·超级链接·商务宴会常用的祝酒词

Commonly-used Expressions for Making A Toast at A Business Banquet

1. Ladies and gentlemen, good evening! First, allow me, on behalf of all the employees of our company, to extend sincere thanks and greetings to all that have come.
2. On behalf of the company, I express sincere thanks and high respect to every leader, every guest, and every friend attending this banquet.
3. Thanks to all who have made time in their busy schedules to attend our banquet.
4. Here's to success at work, health, and the fulfillment of all our wishes! Cheers!
5. Finally, here's to the official establishment of a strong friendship and work partnership, and close collaboration from now on! Cheers!

第 6 课

⊃ 口语任务·网络会议

Sales manager: Hello, to our colleagues in Guangzhou. Can you hear me clearly?

Production manager: It's very clear. Hello, to our colleagues in New York.

Sales manager: We have made a good sale in New York. Can the production support us?

Production manager: We are producing 24 hours a day. I'm sure we can support you.

Sales manager: When can the new goods arrive in New York?

Production manager: This Thursday. We can ensure your sale on the weekend.

Sales manager: I'll contact you after the goods arrive in New York.

Production manager: OK. Talk with you later.

⊃ 拓展·超级链接·企业微信的应用

Using of WeChat Work

As the need for enterprise employees to handle business matters outside of the office has become more and more important, the Tencent corporation launched WeChat Work in 2016. Now enterprise employees can use this phone app to quickly search for business materials needed for work, communicate with co-workers, clock in and out, obtain approval for office procedures, conduct video meetings, and more.

• Address Book: Employees can use the address book to find the contact information for all of the co-workers at the company, and use WeChat Work to communicate with co-workers.

• Video Meeting: Company employees can attend meetings on their phones, and can display documents and share screen.

• Group Chat: Managers can send group chats of up to 2,000 people, post announcements, and ban posts.

• Clock In & Out: Employees can clock in and clock out of work on their phones. Managers can organize the work schedule on their phones, too.

• Report: Employees can report their work progress whenever and wherever possible, and managers can check employees' reports on the phone.

• Examine and Approve: Employees can quickly view and upload office documents. Managers can examine and approve documents on their phones.

第 7 课

⊃ 口语任务·广告的影响力

Salesman: What kind of advertising do you see everyday?

Woman: There are many advertisements on TV,

so I see more television advertising.

Salesman: Sir, what kind of advertising do you see everyday?

Man: I have no time, but I drive everyday. So I listen to some radio advertising.

Salesman: Hey kid, do you like advertisements?

Child: I like them very much. I ask my mum to buy me the tasty food in the advertising.

Salesman: Does the advertising affect your consumption?

Collage student: There is not too much effect. I like to know a product by myself.

⊃ 拓展·超级链接·阿狸的网络营销

Ali the Fox's Online Marketing

Ali the Fox is a well-known original cartoon image in China. Its logo is a cute little fox. Up until now, the sales of Ali the Fox's publications have exceeded 3 million, and the online page has over 10 million registered followers. The success of the Ali brand could not have happened without its outstanding marketing strategies. Ali's author Xu Han says, "The Internet has provided a platform for grassroot cartooners. All people need to do is uploading their work online, and they can gain many viewers." In 2006, he posted the Ali the Fox illustrations on all the major online forums, and also created a set of Ali-themed emojis. From then on, Ali the Fox became an online craze. Ali the Fox has since continued its victorious pursuits and has decided to create and develop Ali-themed products, and sell them through online channels. Thus, Ali the Fox flagship stores have appeared on Taobao, Jingdong and other online platforms. Ali the Fox stuffed animals, Ali the Fox bags, Ali the Fox household products, Ali the Fox clothing and accessories, Ali the Fox books and stationery, and many other items have brought Ali the Fox from the Internet into real life, expanded the market of Ali the Fox, and increased the influence of the brand.

Due to its simple and cute image, Ali the Fox has received high regard from many other brands. Companies such as Macox Lane and KELA have partnered with Ali the Fox, and sell Ali the Fox products regularly. Ali the Fox and these partner brands bring benefits to one another.

第 8 课

⊃ 口语任务·财务预算

Chairman of the board: Have you read the budget plan for next year?

General manager: Yes, I have. I think we should increase the after sale service by 3%.

Chairman of the board: What do you want to do with this money?

General manager: I want to offer an 400 free customer service hotline in order to facilitate communication with the customers.

Chairman of the board: We'll recruit new employees next year, so the human resources expenses must increase too.

General manager: Then we can only reduce the daily administration expense.

Chairman of the board: We need to have a talk with the financial manager.

⊃ 拓展·超级链接·华为的售后服务

Huawei's After-sales Service

As one of the largest mobile phone brands in China, Huawei's success is inseparable from its loyal after-sales services. By the end of 2017, Huawei had built more than 1,400 offline service centers, covering 105 countries and regions around the world. Online services support 65 languages and cover 111 countries and regions around the world. In order to save customers the trouble of having to wait while products are sent to be repaired, Huawei has offered remote maintenance services. In addition, Huawei has also started the "Experience Huawei Service Day" for users to experience Huawei's high-quality service.

Satisfying customers is one of Huawei's core values. Huawei firmly believes that serving customers is the sole reason for Huawei's existence. Customer's demand is the driving force behind Huawei's development. Therefore, Huawei is always customer-centric, responding quickly to customer needs and continuing to create long-term value for its customers. While helping achieve success, Huawei itself has also achieved success.

第 9 课

⊃ 口语任务 · 商业咨询

Entrepreneur: We have already done much research. Now we hope to enter the Guangzhou market.
Consultant: It will be a little easier if you look for a Guangzhou company as your cooperative partner.
Entrepreneur: We can offer the investment, technology and management.
Consultant: In this case, you can look for the ones offer the factory, staff and sales channel.
Entrepreneur: You must know a lot about the local enterprise. Could you give me some recommendations?
Consultant: I can recommend six enterprises to you. They all have their own management or sales advantages.
Entrepreneur: I want to talk with the enterprises which have sales advantages first.
Consultant: I will contact the enterprises at once and arrange your meeting.

⊃ 拓展 · 超级链接 · 麦肯锡大中华公司

McKinsey Greater China

McKinsey's Greater China branch includes five branches in Beijing, Hong Kong, Shanghai, Shenzhen, and Taipei.

In recent years, McKinsey's Greater China branch has successfully launched a series of projects in Greater China, with clients in 15 industries, including national, provincial, and regional governments and institutions. McKinsey's Greater China has provided a wide range of strategic, organizational, and operational consultation services to clients including state-owned enterprises, rapidly growing high-tech companies, leading local financial institutions, and multinational companies in Greater China.

McKinsey Company operates in a "global integration" model that leverages McKinsey's global expertise and external resources to its clients in Greater China.

第 10 课

⊃ 口语任务 · 广告战略

Journalist: In recent years, Adidas' sports shoes have become more and more popular.
Expert: That's because their product design is more and more fashionable.
Journalist: Why?
Expert: Because the design is the important part of sports shoes. Shoes which are not beautiful will never sell.
Journalist: How does the company know the consumers' demands in various countries?
Expert: Adidas is a company with diverse cultures, has nearly 6000 employees from more than 100 countries. They also have design studios in Tokyo and New York and so on.
Journalist: Adidas seems has already changed their advertising strategy.
Expert: Now they invite world-class athletes, actors, singers to represent their brand as well as developed online sales.

⊃ 拓展 · 超级链接 · 阿里巴巴商业生态圈

The Business Ecosystem of Alibaba

In September 2016, Ma Yun and his creation, Alibaba, bought out KFC (China), and became the focus of the news media.

Ma Yun was one of the first entrepreneurs to conduct e-commerce and remain in the world of the Internet in China. He founded the Alibaba Group, which became one of the largest online trade markets and business communication communities in the world in a short time. On September 19, 2014, the Alibaba Group was officially listed on the New York Stock Exchange. On July 19, 2018, the world-famous "Fortune" 500 list was released, and the Alibaba Group was ranked 300.

Alibaba has always been committed to creating a more advanced business ecosystem. Today, Alibaba has grown into a sophisticated business ecosystem with e-commerce as its core mission, with features such as e-commerce finance, local living services, health care, entertainment, and intelligent terminals. The acquisition of KFC (China) may be an important sign that after Alibaba infiltrated and transformed the Internet, banking and logistics industries, it has now crossed into and changed the catering industry, especially the fast food industry.

第 11 课

口语任务 · 不同的企业文化

Tian Le: How is your new job?
Li Yue: Very good. I am very pleased.
Tian Le: Are there some differences from your previous job?
Li Yue: The salary is a little bit lower, but it has good benefits and more opportunities for training.
Tian Le: What about the work and the environment?
Li Yue: Now I have more responsibilities, but the working atmosphere is easier.
Tian Le: My job is so boring. The cooperation between departments is not good. Some of my colleagues have already quit the job.
Li Yue: Different companies have different culture. If you cannot accept the culture of your company, you should consider changing your job.
Tian Le: A headhunting company has been in contact with me.
Li Yue: Income and the working environment are very important. So you must consider them well.

拓展 · 超级链接 · 腾讯的企业文化

The Company Culture of Tencent

Founded in 1988, Shenzhen Tencent Computer System Co., Ltd. is one of the largest Internet integrated service providers in China. In 2017, Tencent ranked 47th among the world's top 500 brands.

Tencent has always been committed to being the most popular Internet company, constantly listening closely to and satisfying user needs, enhancing the brand image, promoting the common development of the Internet industry, focusing on corporate responsibility, and gaining universal respect from users, employees, the industry and society. Tencent hopes to enhance people's quality of life through the Internet, and to provide conveniences and enjoyment to people through personalized and humanized services.

Tencent has a thorough internal talent training system, so that employees can choose the training category that suits them at different stages of their career development, and combine their strengths and interests to choose the development channel that suits them. Tencent tries to provide employees with a better and more powerful learning environment and atmosphere, which is also a favorable factor which helps Tencent attract and retain employees.

Tencent has a special public welfare platform — Tencent Public Welfare. The total amount of donations overtime has reached 4.6 billion yuan. Tencent has also won the China Charity Award for two consecutive years in 2011 and 2012, making great contributions to the cause of public welfare.

第 12 课

口语任务 · 慈善拍卖筹备

Chairman: How is the charity auction gala you prepared going?
Manager: The Chinese calligraphy, painting and craftwork for the auction have already been prepared.

Chairman: I am sure they are very artistic.
Manager: Yes, the income of this auction can help at least one hundred poor college students complete their study.
Chairman: Have you contacted the banquet hall at the Beijing Hotel?
Manager: Yes, we have. We have invited Mr. Fang, the famous auctioneer to host the auction.
Chairman: You should send invitations to all the clients, and confirm one by one by phone.
Manager: Many people are interested in this charity auction. 80% of them have confirmed that they will attend.

 拓展 · 超级链接 · 万达的企业使命

Wanda Group's Corporate Mission

The mission of China's Wanda Group is to "create wealth together and serve society". The chairman of the Wanda Group once said, "The development of Wanda is not only for itself, but also for society; the wealth created from Wanda's endeavors will eventually be given back to society."

In terms of social welfare, since its inception in 1988, Wanda Group has invested more than 5.8 billion yuan in social charity. Projects include constructing kindergartens, primary schools and middle schools; donations to earthquake disaster relief projects such as Wenchuan and Yushu; China's soccer revival, restoration of cultural sites, and beyond. Wanda Group has won awards such as the National China Charity Award and the Poverty Eradication Award multiple times.

In terms of job creation, the Wanda Group has become a national leading enterprise for employment in the past several years. In order to encourage university students to start their own businesses, Wanda Group has also launched a 10-year plan to support university student entrepreneurship, and is setting up career service departments to provide professional guidance to university students.

In addition, the Wanda Group is the first company in the country to promote energy-efficient buildings.

郑重声明

高等教育出版社依法对本书享有专有出版权。任何未经许可的复制、销售行为均违反《中华人民共和国著作权法》，其行为人将承担相应的民事责任和行政责任；构成犯罪的，将被依法追究刑事责任。为了维护市场秩序，保护读者的合法权益，避免读者误用盗版书造成不良后果，我社将配合行政执法部门和司法机关对违法犯罪的单位和个人进行严厉打击。社会各界人士如发现上述侵权行为，希望及时举报，本社将奖励举报有功人员。

反盗版举报电话　（010）58581999　58582371　58582488
反盗版举报传真　（010）82086060
反盗版举报邮箱　dd@hep.com.cn
通信地址　北京市西城区德外大街4号　高等教育出版社法律事务与版权管理部
邮政编码　100120

图书在版编目（CIP）数据

体验汉语短期教程. 商务篇：英语版 / 张红，岳薇主编. -- 修订本. -- 北京：高等教育出版社，2019.3
ISBN 978-7-04-051010-2

Ⅰ. ①体… Ⅱ. ①张… ②岳… Ⅲ. ①汉语—对外汉语教学—教材 Ⅳ. ①H195.4

中国版本图书馆CIP数据核字（2019）第006848号

策划编辑	梁　宇	责任编辑	杨　曦	封面设计	张　楠	版式设计	水长流文化
英文审译	Jeremy Rubinstein, Lyric Grimes	插图选配	杨　曦	责任校对	李　玮	责任印制	尤　静

出版发行	高等教育出版社	网　　址	http://www.hep.edu.cn
社　　址	北京市西城区德外大街4号		http://www.hep.com.cn
邮政编码	100120	网上订购	http://www.hepmall.com.cn
印　　刷	北京鑫丰华彩印有限公司		http://www.hepmall.com
开　　本	889mm×1194mm 1/16		http://www.hepmall.cn
印　　张	7.75		
字　　数	240千字	版　　次	2019年3月第1版
购书热线	010-58581118	印　　次	2019年3月第1次印刷
咨询电话	400-810-0598	定　　价	68.00元

本书如有缺页、倒页、脱页等质量问题，请到所购图书销售部门联系调换
版权所有　侵权必究
物　料　号　51010-00